I'VE FINISI

SO I'LL ST.

For a complete list of Management Books 2000 titles
visit our web-site on http://www.mb2000.com

I'VE FINISHED, SO I'LL START

A guide to a full and active retirement

Stephen Howarth and John Houghton

Illustrations by Dan Marsden

2000

First published in 2006 by Management Books 2000 Ltd
Forge House, Limes Road
Kemble, Cirencester
Gloucestershire, GL7 6AD, UK
Tel: 0044 (0) 1285 771441
Fax: 0044 (0) 1285 771055
Email: info@mb2000.com
Web: www.mb2000.com

Printed and bound in Great Britain by Direct-POD, Northampton – www.direct-pod.com

British Library Cataloguing in Publication Data is available

ISBN 9781852525392

Contents

Acknowledgements

We are grateful to Brian Hunt of Ebor Asset Management for providing the "budget planner" printed on page 112 and the "risk strategy" table printed on page 113.

Introduction
The End of the Beginning

If you have picked up this book to read, then you are probably not in the first flush of youth. The innocent years are behind you. You will probably pride yourself that you can remember the second verse of one of 10cc's or the Kinks' hit singles. You happily wander around singing

'One of sixteen vestal virgins, leaving for the coast'

from Procul Harum's *Whiter Shade of Pale* and still not have the faintest idea what it means.

You will recall a time when a group from Newcastle, who had probably never been outside Tyneside, topped the charts on both sides of the Atlantic. They sang in a kind of Geordie/Mid-Atlantic accent about a house in New Orleans. Just what were the Animals singing about in *The House of the Rising Sun*? Surely it was not just an advert for the local sushi bar; it was a bit premature for that. If it was about a bordello, 'rising sun' must be one of the most obscure metaphors ever used. At that time you couldn't care less.

You were around during the sixties and enjoyed every minute of it, although if you're like me, 'flower power', drug orgies and love-ins seemed to bypass your street.

You know by heart the players and positions of your favourite football team and their fleeting moments of glory. You can remember Dan Dare and the *Wizard* and can recall bit actors in British B movies.

The girls will remember beehive hairstyles, wasp belts, balloon skirts, sack dresses, the joy of Mary Quant's innovations, hot pants, black Sobranie cigarettes, Dansette record players, Radio Luxembourg and Tab Hunter. Nylon stockings and suspender belts will have fond memories for both sexes, perhaps for different reasons.

You will be able to recall exactly where you were and what you were doing when John F. Kennedy was assassinated, and when Armstrong took his giant step for mankind on the moon and you will remember every dance routine ever performed by Pan's People.

Does this ring a bell with you? Then you will probably be someone who will regale any remotely interested audience about the joys of listening to the wireless on Sunday afternoon – Billy Cotton's Bandshow, Hancock's Half-Hour and the surreal Educating Archie, when you never considered the bizarre concept of a ventriloquist working on radio. You will never know just how good or bad Peter Brough was.

You know the names of those three old women who used to meet in the snug of the Rover's Return, and you can remember the name of the host in *Take Your Pick*. Do you feel that *Tomorrow's World* was never the same after Raymond Baxter left?

When mature actors or actresses appear on the television these days, you probably nudge your partner and say something like, 'She's looking a bit rough,' or, 'He's let himself go,' as you

At this age even the policemen start to look younger…

slump, dishevelled on your favourite couch. Do you find that some of the women in *Last of the Summer Wine* are becoming faintly attractive?

You are probably in the afternoon of your life or you may well be sitting down to an early tea. You are constantly saying, 'Doesn't time fly?' – and as the old joke goes, when you bend down to tie your shoelaces, you look around for other things to do while you

9

are down there. You seem to have another birthday every three months.

When you go to a restaurant, you probably can't read the menu, you can't hear the specials and even then you ask the waiter to repeat them because you couldn't remember them.

Do you embarrass your children when you get up to dance at parties and do what you think is a really cool version of 'the Locomotion'? You probably play a mean air guitar with especial dexterity on the riffs in Buddy Holly's *Peggy Sue* and Eric Clapton's *Layla*.

The Bee Gees' *Staying Alive* is starting to take on a new significance for you.

When you meet new people these days they invariably remind you of somebody you have already met.

You may well be considering a change of lifestyle, if indeed you have not already made the decision. You have a feeling that there must be more to life. You may well have been associated (I won't say 'worked') with the same organisation for a good number of years.

In their wisdom, in addition to the whisky decanters and the gold watch, they may well be donating you a substantial amount of money so that you will leave them, in the mistaken belief they can be more effective without your services. They have planned to give your job to some less experienced, less able person. They will give it to someone half your age, who will work for half as much and do half the work.

If you are indeed this person, then this is the book for you. It is time to put on one of the pairs of glasses that you don't really need, if you can remember where you put them down, and read on.

You must not read any other publication that purports to be a guide to retirement. We have read them all for you.

Their main message is that you should look after your money, eat healthy foods and get out of the house more. Big deal! They are patronising, prescriptive and incredibly boring.

The majority seem to be compiled by people in their 30s, who really should get a life of their own before they start advising others.

But this book is not a mumbo-jumbo lifestyle book. It is not 'Chicken Soup for the Bewildered' or 'Seven Effective Habits for Highly Incontinent People'. Neither is it a cheesy 'You-are-your-cardigan-and-slippers' or 'You-are-sausages-and-mash' theory, emanating from some pompous lifestyle guru. It is not a 'Men are from Glasgow, women are from Edinburgh' manual.

Whilst the tone is light-hearted, we will touch upon some serious issues, like finance, health, age in culture, society and politics, but the plan is to destroy the various myths that surround 'life after work' and concentrate on the myriad positive aspects.

The Spanish word for a retired person is *jubilador* and the very next word on the next line in the Spanish dictionary is *jubilo* which means 'joy' and 'rejoicing'. It is this closeness of these two words, which could be considered the main theme of this book.

'I have been through some terrible things in my life, some of which actually happened.'

Mark Twain

11

Light the Blue Touch Paper

'Something Happened' by Joseph Heller

'People in the company are almost never fired. If they grow inadequate or obsolete ahead of schedule, they are eased aside into hollow, insignificant, newly created positions with fake functions and no authority, where they are sheepish and unhappy for as long as they remain. Nearly always, they must occupy a small and less convenient office, sometimes one with another person already in it. If they are still relatively young, they are simply encouraged directly (although with courtesy) to find jobs with other companies and they resign.'

The concept of 'retirement', as we know it, is a relatively modern term. The original concept of a retirement age of 65 was introduced by Bismarck in the 1880s when life expectancy was 45. It was not put into practice in the UK until the latter part of the 20th century. Prior to this, men, in particular, usually shuffled off this mortal coil whilst they were still fully employed. Life expectancy was shorter and the period after work was relatively brief.

Nowadays, with the improvement in medical and health care, improved economic conditions, healthier diets and more opportunities for exercise, life expectancy has improved, and is expected to increase markedly. At the turn of the century in the Western world, men were expected to live until they were 60 at the most, and women to 70. Now, that has been extended to 75 for men and 80 for women.

As a result of this demographic shift, there exists a whole new stratum of society, consisting of people who have finished work, and are fit and economically sound. A stratum of society that did not exist 20 or 30 years ago. Their children have left the nest and they have large amounts of time on their hands.

What is more this may be only a temporary state of affairs, as the retirement age is pushed back, and pension savings become harder to accrue. It is generally accepted that in the future, younger people will no longer have the opportunity of staying with one organisation for 20 or 30 years. In the private sector, with whatever name is given to it, re-structuring, de-layering, downsizing, 'youthanasia' or outsourcing, organisations are no longer in a position to offer employees the kind of security and longevity of employment enjoyed by the current batch of retirees.

Indeed, the current view is that people will change their jobs some nine times over their working life. As a consequence, they will not be in a position to accrue any substantial amounts in company pensions. They may also be swamped in the muddy waters of private pensions.

With the problem of the ageing society, where the numbers of retired workers will exceed the numbers of the people actually working, the provision of a national pension will become problematic. People will be encouraged or indeed forced to work, whilst they still have the fading ability to hold a pen, see a computer screen or hear the telephone ringing.

And so, this could be termed the 'Golden Age' for people in a certain condition – people who have had a successful career in the occupational sense and are about to embark upon this remarkable journey into the world of 'Life after Work'.

Many people look forward to this transition with a great sense of relief. They anticipate a release from the stresses and strains of organisational existence, the daily aggravation of insecure managers, inept colleagues and irate customers.

This was illustrated quite graphically on a recent project, in which we were involved.

There were plans to downsize the Prison service and many

Prison Officers were given the opportunity to take early retirement. The project involved visiting Her Majesty's prisons and providing support for the people who were considering leaving the service. In a particular open prison, we had to pass through a kind of recreation room for the inmates. On the wall was a calendar where the inmates were crossing off each day and counting the days till their release.

We then went into the Prison Officers quarters and there on the wall was the same calendar, with the same crossings, where the officers were crossing off the days to their retirement. A rather sad state of affairs.

The reality is that most people will not miss their working environment. If they have spent any length of time with an organisation, they will invariably have started to experience a sense of 'déjâ vu', as one after another reorganisation and change initiative flows through the ranks. They will probably have experienced the joys of Management by Objectives, Total Quality Management, Business Process Re-engineering, Benchmarking, World Class Performance and goodness knows what, as each new generation of acne-ridden managers endeavour to assert their own self-serving values and ambitions on a somewhat sceptical workforce.

The current breed of managers seems a strange group of mirthless automatons, inhabiting a nether world of mission statements and core values – a surreal world where playing fields are not level; where goalposts are prone to being moved; where boxes need to be thought outside of, and envelopes need to be pushed.

This soulless group of individuals seem to have been fed on a diet of airport management books purporting to contain the alchemy of business success. A diet of gimmickry and gobbledegook produced mainly by American gurus all peddling the secrets of success liberally sprinkled with platitudes and jargon. A simple crowd who probably think Churchill was the founder of the insurance business.

Many people retiring now will have worked with the kind of organisation that has one Statement of Purpose, one Vision, five Values, six goals, seven Strategic Priorities and eight Key Performance Indicators, without any clear correlation between them. A recipe for total confusion and exasperation.

Experienced people may well have had to bite their tongues as initiatives that have palpably failed miserably in the past, are wheeled out again and re-introduced in a different guise, sacrifices on the altar of the Great God of Organisational Change.

A ludicrous example is the current vogue for organisations spending enormous budgets and changing their name to one word, usually either starting or ending in the letter 'A'. This completely mystifies customers and employees alike. Does anybody now remember who 'Consignia' were?

Another scurrilous example is from the banking industry. Where previously you could go into your local branch and go about your business quietly and efficiently. These branches have now been transformed into Middle Eastern souks, with all sorts of unsavoury characters trying to sell you a wide range of questionable products. And if you do have a serious problem, you are routed to a call-centre where you need to enlist the help of some poor person in the Southern Hemisphere, or Cardiff, whose knowledge of financial matters probably extends to last week's issue of the DailyTelegraph.

Most of these initiatives are dreamed up by pre-pubescent

marketing executives at brainstorming exercises in the afternoon after a tofu, quorn and caffeine-fuelled lunch.

The great sadness is, of course, that if anyone actually energises themselves enough and has the temerity to question these developments, and to point out the obvious shortcomings, then this person immediately is tagged as being 'resistant to change'. A tick goes in the wrong box on the Annual Appraisal form. They are ostracised, branded as a Luddite and vilified in the company canteen and in the local café bars and bistros.

"The trouble with you, Carruthers, is that you cannot adapt to change"

There are a number of reasons why people decide to leave the asylum to the inmates.

People always come to this decision from a unique perspective. They approach from different financial perspectives, from different family perspectives, from different backgrounds, they all have different hopes and dreams. There are money concerns, concerns about loss of status and identity, concern about the implications of having all this extra time on their hands, concerns about a lack of structure in their life.

Some people want to spend more time with their family; some people want to spend more time with somebody else's family. It does seem important that any decision to take early retirement really should focus on the positive aspects of the condition. The people who seem to make the greatest success of the transition are the people who do not look upon retirement as a closing down, or a slowing down. They look upon it as a life-changing regeneration and they embrace all the opportunities that this freedom allows. It is a matter of choices. Retirement is a transition not a transformation.

One thing is certain. Once you have made the decision to retire and it becomes known throughout the organisation, then, almost overnight, you become 'yesterday's man'. Colleagues avert their eyes in the corridors. Social chitchat immediately ceases when you enter the room. There is intense speculation from junior colleagues as to who will be your replacement. When you tell people, you will see their eyes glaze over masking sometimes admiration but almost always pity. You will be approached by mere acquaintances, who seem obsessed with your future plans and ask incessant questions like, 'But what are you going to do?'

Another ritual to be prepared for is the retirement lunch that may well be organised in your honour. You should really be prepared to gnaw off your left foot before agreeing to this humiliation. They are excruciatingly embarrassing for all concerned.

The false bonhomie, the transparent insincerity and the empty platitudes really have no place outside a meeting of the current Cabinet and should be avoided at all costs.

I especially recall a particularly excruciating example of the Retirement Lunch, I attended a few years ago.

It was with a major oil company and one of the chaps who had worked in the accounts office decided to retire after thirty-three years with the company. A lunch at a local hostelry was duly arranged for him.

The person, who had drawn the short straw and so had to make the presentation speech, was one of the more callow executives who had absolutely no knowledge of the retiree's career, background, family circumstances, or anything else about him.

On the short walk from the office to the hotel, I had to brief the executive on all these matters – like the fact that his wife had recently died, so to refer to his other half would be inappropriate; the fact that he had driven a tank at the Normandy landings; what roles he had fulfilled during this lifetime with the company, what he liked to do in his spare time and other relevant anecdotes.

To be fair, the lad made a decent fist of the presentation speech, but embarrassment was heaped upon embarrassment as he kept referring to the chap as 'John' this...and 'John' that... 'Good old John.'

At the end of the presentation, he turned to the chap and said 'You don't mind me calling you John, do you?'

The chap replied rather icily, 'No, you can call me anything you want. But my name is Jim'.

Another rule for the retired person is that you must never attend any official or semi-official reunions. By all means have a few pints occasionally with some of your closest friends. But you must never return to any company functions whatsoever.

You are definitely 'yesterday's man' and will be treated like the Ancient Mariner or Banquo's ghost. You are an embarrassment to them and all they want to tell you is how bad it has become since you left. Resist strongly any invitations 'to keep in touch' and it is definitely time to head for the exit when they start saying 'You certainly went at the right time.'

There is an excruciating sequence in the superb film *About Schmidt.* Jack Nicholson plays the part of an insurance executive who has retired. There is a gut-wrenching farewell lunch and after a week, he decides to pay a visit to his old office to see if he can be of any help to his successor.

The young brash successor gives him short shrift and as he is leaving he sees the files from the project he has been working on for the last five years dumped in the trash can.

Painful. But the truth hurts.

You will certainly miss many aspects of corporate life, but we need to look at this in a bit more depth. You will miss the myopic, old, Mr Grace approach: 'You are all doing very well,' from the senior echelons of management. You will miss the Machiavellian antics, bullying and paranoia of some middle managers. You will miss the frenetic amiability of the Sales Department and the unctuous bonhomie of the Marketing Department. You will miss the greyness and suspicion of the Finance Department and their sinister shock troopers, the Auditors.

You will miss the 'We are one, big happy family' mantra from the self-seekers in the Human Resource Department, and the Mary Poppins inhabitants of the Training Department. But above all, you will miss the *'Have you tried switching it on? The Computer says No'* counsel from the droogs on the Help desk in the IT Department.

You will miss the interminable meetings, where minutes are taken and hours lost with those mind-numbing, will–sapping Powerpoint presentations. The acute embarrassment of the Annual Appraisal meeting.

You will miss the posters on the wall proclaiming 'People are our greatest asset' in offices where people are treated like medieval serfs. The 'Customer is King' posters in offices where any call from the aforementioned customer is answered with irritation and disdain, where any request from the customer, however simple, is treated like a demand to solve the mysteries of the universe. You will miss the younger members of the management team, always prepared to give people the full benefits of their inexperience.

You will miss the excruciating Christmas parties, where arch enemies, fuelled with free alcohol suddenly metamorphose into 'besht friends'. Female employees are subjected to slobbering harassment. They have to cleverly divert and brush off these approaches when all the blokes want to do is get into their skirts. They need to be diplomatic and not to offend the drunks too much; otherwise their life for the next year becomes hell.

You may also miss the nauseous feeling that starts creeping over you just after *Songs of Praise* on a Sunday evening, when it dawns on you that the weekend is over and another week of stress and frustration awaits you in the morning.

All sadly missed.

People say 'Never go back', and it is particularly appropriate in this situation. Of course, it is nice to remember the three good times you have had over the past twenty years but the healthy attitude seems to be to make a clean break and concentrate on the rich new experiences that await you.

> 'For a long time it seemed to me that life was about to begin. Real life. But there was always some obstacle in the way, something to be gotten through first, some unfinished business, time still to be served, a debt to be paid. At last it dawned on me that these obstacles are my life.'
>
> *Alfred de Souza*

APPROACHING RETIREMENT QUIZ

	TRUE	PARTLY TRUE	NOT TRUE
I believe I can add years to my life.	____	____	____
I am aware of the effect on my family of my decision.	____	____	____
My suits have come back into fashion.	____	____	____
I have developed a plan for my retirement years.	____	____	____
My working colleagues refer to me as 'Uncle'.	____	____	____
On my office door, my name and title are written in chalk.	____	____	____
I have been through four re-organisations.	____	____	____
I have discussed this with my spouse (or partner) and we have mutually developed a plan for our future.	____	____	____
I have considered how I am going to spend this substantial increase in leisure time.	____	____	____
I am aware of the effect my health regime will have in the future.	____	____	____
I am more of an action man than a thinker.	____	____	____

If your ticks are mainly down the 'True' column then perhaps it is time to light the blue touch paper and retire.

2

Who Needs Work?

As one prepares for life after work, it always a useful exercise to take one step back and consider why one ever went to work in the first place. Why did you ever force yourself out of a warm bed on a freezing February morning, brave the squalid commuter journey or the infuriating traffic jams to arrive panting at a workplace, inhabited with cyberskivers, and apathetic, work-shy colleagues?

You remained there for anything up to ten hours each day and then dragged yourself home, ate a nondescript evening meal, and then slumped in front of the television for night after night. Why did you do this?

There are many sacrifices to be made on the altar of a career, most of which are made to false and malicious gods.

When any discussion about motivation at work crops up, sociologists wheel out Maslow's Hierarchy of Needs theory, which is an elegant explanation of some of the reasons why people work.

Maslow poses a hierarchy of needs in which as soon as one

level of need is satisfied, then people move to a higher level. Hence the hierarchy.

Most people when questioned maintain that their sole reason for working at all was 'Money'. Certainly, paid employment satisfies the two basic needs for survival and security. People exchange their time and energy for money, which enables them to purchase the basic food and liquid nourishment that keep body and soul together.

Once they are in a position where they no longer have to worry each day where the next meal is coming from, then they move to the next level of need, which is the need for Security. They need to achieve a buffer, where they are no longer confronting a daily life-threatening situation. Long-term employment satisfies this need for security. Regular salaries, benefits, and the promise of pensions seem to fit the bill for most people in the satisfaction of their security needs.

The entire financial, insurance and banking sector is there to fuel and exploit this level of need. Savings schemes, the provision of mortgages, pension planning and insurance programmes are all created to pander to and exploit these needs. People are attracted to these invitations, because they offer a chance to insulate themselves from the 'slings and arrows' of every day living.

Once these two basis physical needs are satisfied then we move to the next level.

Many people report that one of the main reasons for working is that it gets them out of the house and meeting other people. One of the main things they consider they will miss in retirement will be their friends and colleagues at work. They like the exchange of ideas, the camaraderie and their close relationships with colleagues.

This is the next level of need, which is more psychological than economic. Man is a gregarious animal. We need to 'belong'; we need the cut and thrust of the exchange of ideas. We like the 'crack' and the general stimulation provided by the group.

Generally, we like to associate with people, who are fundamentally like ourselves. We like conformity and harmony in our relationships.

After all, as a punishment we put criminals and wrongdoers in 'solitary confinement' where they are isolated and their senses are deprived of this stimulation.

This need is manipulated and exploited by organisations in the constant drive and insistence of teamwork. In the main, organisations do not like 'mavericks'. They do not encourage the 'free thinkers'. They like conformists; they ostracise people who 'rock the boat'. They promote teamwork, mediocrity and conformity. Why do they do this? The simple fact is that it is easier to control.

If you visited the boardrooms and higher echelons of any major organisation and considered who was present. The chances are that there are very few team players at these heady heights. Teamwork is all right for the lower reaches but at the top every one is in it for themselves. Just look at successful politicians and the captains of industry and judge whether they are good team players or not. Thatcher, Blair, Bush, Murdoch, Greene, Branson, Maxwell, Hitler and anybody else we do not afford the courtesy of their first name – the list goes on and on.

Speaking to Michael Parkinson, Michael Winner, successful film-maker and gourmet famously said, 'I think teamwork is great!! It is a bunch of people doing what I tell them to do.'

Nevertheless, people do have this need to belong, and working with people who you admire and can relate to is a very positive state of affairs.

Once this need is satisfied, then we move on to the next level, which is a need for Status, a sense of identity and self-esteem. Some people, although they are part of the group, want to show that somehow they are doing better than the group.

They buy a bigger car or house – the 'keeping ahead of the Joneses' syndrome.

They pursue higher financial rewards, they join the right clubs and they spend all their energies climbing the greasy pole of promotions and self-advancement.

Once again, this need is exploited in organisations, by the proliferation of executive toilets, dining rooms and car parking spaces, the size of offices and even the depth of the pile on the office carpet – and the many different job titles that abound, each vying with each other to convey the highest levels of achievement.

Whilst many people are not overtly driven by such motives, nevertheless people define themselves by their occupation. Many people do relish the sense of identity and importance their status at work affords them. Working for an international company, a company with a household name, or a particularly successful company in the private sector, does, by association, reflect the importance and status of the individual. Obviously to have a distinct profession does generate a certain amount of social status. Senior positions in the public sector, in local government, the medical profession, the police force and in the educational system all carry their own distinct kudos.

The highest and the final level in Maslow's hierarchy is what he calls the need for 'self-actualisation'. If you can tick this box as well, you are somehow in a supreme state of being – all your needs have been fully met, all your potential has been fulfilled; you are recognised and rewarded and in a complete state of happiness.

Strangely enough, one does not meet too many people working in organisations who achieve this elevated state. There is a widely held view that organisations only use 10% of anybody's ability anyway. Vast reservoirs of talent and ability are never tapped.

Enormous tracts of creativity and imagination are not cultivated and left fallow.

There are, of course, exceptions. Occasionally, one will come upon a nurse or a teacher, for example, who might exude this kind of self-fulfilment, and it is true that some people *do* achieve a portion of this higher level of fulfilment through work, but for the majority this sense of fulfilment is achieved outside the work place.

For most people, their employment satisfies their economic and social needs and yet their true fulfilment is met outside their occupational role.

Many people seek inner fulfilment in their family situation. It comes from spending more quality time with their families. There is a balance between their working life and their family life. They take great interest and delight in the activities and achievements of their children and other members of the family.

Others derive this satisfaction from travelling. They avidly plan their annual holidays, months in advance. They anticipate the joys of the journey. They are at their happiest visiting different locations and studying different cultures and ways of life.

Others derive this satisfaction from sport and hobbies. They give their allegiance to their favourite football team. They are part of other sporting teams and associations. The golfers, tennis players and fell walkers all derive great satisfaction from playing or watching their favourite sporting pastimes.

Then there are the DIY'ers and the gardeners, they spend many long, enriching hours, renovating houses, laying patios and cultivating their flowers, vegetables and plants.

Others derive this satisfaction from self-development and further education. They become involved in a wide range of educational activities from taking learning a second language at evening classes to taking a fully-fledged degree through the Open University.

Wherever this satisfaction comes from, it does seem to emanate from activities outside the workplace. It seems that many people are prepared to sell their time, expertise and energy to achieve a certain level of financial security. Real fulfilment and enjoyment are afforded a lower priority and elbowed out to the margins.

With the prospect of retirement, we need to return and look at the situation through Maslow's prism. The whole situation is totally reversed and turned on its head (see the diagram opposite).

Provided that people feel financially secure there is no need to spend 40 hours a week trying to achieve financial reward.

Their total time and energy can be spent fulfilling these needs of self-realisation and actualisation. OK. Fine, we do need to feel comfortable about money, and health is the joker in the pack, but retirement is the greatest of opportunities to cast off this yoke to concentrate on aspects of our life which give us the greatest satisfaction, enjoyment and happiness.

This truth is central to the issue and people who have successful periods in retirement are the people who grasp this wholeheartedly and are prepared to put it into positive action.

Maslow's Hierarchy of Needs

	AT WORK	AFTER WORK
Self Actualisation	++++	++++++++++++++++++++
Status	++++++++	+++++++++++++++++
Belonging	+++++++++++++	+++++++++++++
Security	+++++++++++++++++	++++++++
Survival	++++++++++++++++++++++	++++

A continuum from 'Having' through 'Doing' to 'Being'

Another way of looking at it is that everybody operates within their own 'comfort zone', a kind of psychological bubble or blanket in which they envelop themselves.

Inside the bubble it is very warm and, of course, very comfortable. It is very secure and predictable.

The roots of the development of the comfort zone can probably be attributed to early childhood. If you had a normal family upbringing, then it was your parents, especially your mother, who provided this shield of protection. You will undoubtedly recall your mother's voice saying things like 'Don't go too near the fire', 'Don't cross the road' and 'Come on home, when it starts to get dark'.

She was there to protect you, to ward off any danger and to support and comfort you.

It is a very pleasant sense of reassurance.

There are some schools of thought which maintain that when you grow up you choose a partner who provides you with the same sense of security and reassurance. Whilst this may be hotly debated in some circles, there is no doubt that many people choose a job, a career or an occupation, which affords them this sense of security and comfort.

The salary or wages, the regular income, the benefits, the comfortable working location, the pleasant colleagues are the tangible trappings of this comfort zone.

People who have worked in one organisation for considerable periods of time have certainly been operating within their comfort zones.

With the prospect of retirement and leaving this zone, people are propelled to the very edge of their comfort zone. They are being asked to leave the certainty and safety the organisation has provided for a long period of time. It is perfectly normal to feel a little apprehensive about the world outside the zone. It is full of uncertainties and imponderables. Questions like, 'Will I have enough money?', 'How will I spend my time?', 'How will friends and family react to my new status?', are perfectly sensible.

Herein lies the great opportunity. What lies outside the comfort zone is exactly what you make it.

Ok so it has been comfortable in there. But it hasn't been very stimulating, there hasn't been much excitement, you have never really tested yourself. Whenever any decision has been made, it was always the comfortable option that was chosen.

You are now approaching a state of freedom and independence. No longer at the mercy of the David Brents of this world, no longer crushed by bureaucracy and inefficiency, now is the time to start living.

It is at this stage that people's attitude has an immense impact on the course this journey will take. If they consider that this is a time for withdrawing, for slowing down – if they consider that they are too old to adapt to any changes – if they approach everything outside their comfort zone with suspicion and apprehension, then they will undoubtedly endure an unfulfilling time in their life after work.

If, however, they approach this period with a positive attitude, considering it to be a time of challenge, to broaden their horizons, to have confidence in their own experience and wisdom, then this will be one of the most enriching and fruitful journeys of their whole existence.

The Comfort Zone

Risk		Excitement
Uncertainty		Change
Worry	Security	Growth
Fear	Comfort	Opportunity
Failure	Warmth	Challenge
Loss	Predictable	Gain
Rigid		Adaptable
Decline		Future

$\overline{\underline{3}}$

You Are Not Old Till You Lose All Your Marvels

Every person approaches the prospect of retirement from their own unique perspective. People come from different backgrounds, different family situations, different financial circumstances, different hopes and different dreams. That is why it is a fruitless exercise to try to prescribe a general course of action for everyone. It is rather like being presented with a basket of fruit. If you like bananas, you take them. If you like apples, you take the apples and leave the rest. No two people are the same.

One of the problems associated with this stage of life is the very use of the word 'retirement'. The root of the word is 'tire' and this conjures up images of 'tiredness', 'slowing down', 'withdrawing' and 'ceasing to be involved'. Sportsmen 'retire' from competitions because they have suffered an injury. Formula One drivers 'retire' from the race because their car has ceased to function. In the dictionary 'to retire' is defined as 'to give up, to go away, to seek seclusion, recede or disappear.'

However the Chinese symbol for crisis, *wei chi,* is the same as the symbol for opportunity, and in actual fact the word 'retirement' should be closer in origin to other words like, 're-juvenate', 're-invigorate', and 're-generate' and other hyphenated words, which imply a renewal and an introduction of a second wind. Perhaps resurrection is one of the most significant words in the English language.

In an occupational sense, retirement is irrevocably linked with advanced age and the ageing process. In western society, age and the ageing process have negative connotations. It must be stressed that this attitude is unique to westernised, industrialised nations. Maturity is treated in a diametrically opposed fashion in more traditional societies.

In the more traditional cultures of the Mediterranean, the Middle East, Japan and China, the elders of the family are revered and respected for their wisdom and experience. They are brought into the centre of family activity. Their views are highly regarded. They command respect and no family decision is taken without consulting them and taking their viewpoints into consideration. There is an African saying that illustrates a healthy attitude to the generation gap: 'If your elders take care of you, while you are cutting your teeth, you must in turn take care of them when they are losing theirs.' Nursing homes, senior centres and assisted living communities are unknown concepts in these societies.

In the so called civilized western world, once an individual is perceived as being unable to perform a role which provides economic advancement for the capitalist machine, then they are discarded and devalued at the first opportunity. They are ostracised and hidden away and as soon as they start slavering a little, failing to find their mouths with their food and start momentarily forgetting names and places, they are whisked into a home for the bewildered without their feet touching the ground.

In other cultures maturity, experience and wisdom are highly regarded. Sadly, in ours these qualities are undervalued and even ignored.

Why should this be so? Well there is no getting away from it. We do live in a society obsessed with youth and the young. The people that most influence our views, tastes and perceived needs are the young – the pre-pubescent marketing executives and the youthful 'twenty-something' media operators. It is a fact that over half of all the people working in the advertising and media businesses are under thirty.

Millions of pounds are spent on advertising directed at the

young, targeting their immature doubts and innermost fears. There are many unwritten rules. They must wear clothes that attract other young people. They must buy the cosmetics and perfumes that make them attractive. They must drink the same drinks, or they will be outsiders without friends. Appearance is valued over substance. No wonder there are so many psychological and social problems with young people when they are bombarded with these messages at a particularly unsettling period of their lives.

The media is obsessed with the cult of youth and transient celebrity. Ours is a strange society where people will pay good money for the autobiography of some pimply, dough-faced twenty-year-old footballer who has only just started eating solid foods and has only recently mastered the ability to perform his own bodily functions without parental assistance.

It seems that the only occasion when age-related topics appear in the media is when inexperienced thirty-somethings refer to older people as though they are some separate social entity. They refer to 'them', 'their situation' and 'their needs'. There is certainly no shortage of publicity regarding problems with misdemeanours in care homes, the pensions crisis and the possibility of a cure for Alzheimer's disease – hardly the more attractive aspects of becoming older.

'No napkins....elderly might eat them.'

Guardian Headline – April 2005

Another aspect of this false impression is that in addition to the media being dominated by sallow youths, any academic studies into age, the ageing process and gerontology seem to be conducted by people of similar attitudes, totally lacking any empathy with mature people. For the purposes of their studies, mature people are categorised as if they were some kind of exotic tribe.

Some medical people, particularly the owners of care homes, have vested interests in treating mature people as a distinctly separate section of society.

Perhaps the more militant among us could consider ageism to be in the same category as racism and sexism was a number of years ago – a deliberate attempt to marginalise and withdraw opportunity from a distinct section of society. Afternoon television is a case in point. The advertisers know their market. For the unemployed there are scores of commercials about debt consolidation agencies and for the mature person there are commercials for walk-in baths, staircase lifts and cures for incontinence.

It is not only in the media that older people get a bad press. In literature also, this negative image is perpetuated. After all, King Lear, Humbert Humbert, Miss Havisham, Don Quixote and Scrooge are not the sort of people you would invite as guests to your dinner party for their scintillating conversation and *joie de vivre*.

As a consequence of this pandering to the youth-obsessed market, sadly some mature people try and camouflage their own ageing process. They buy cosmetics, undergo painful medical treatments and wear various prosthetics in an attempt to mask or even hide the natural ageing process.

The harsh fact is that ageing occurs to everyone without exception, so you need to get on with it. OK – if a face-lift, wearing a wig, or a Botox injection makes you feel better in yourself, then by all means do it. But if your motive is merely to try and appear years younger than you really are to satisfy a media stereotype, then forget it.

It is time for mature people (and let's bear in mind there are more of us than them) to strike back and redress the imbalance in this misinformation. We should emphasise the positive aspects of ageing at every occasion: the beauty of age; the benefits of rich experience and accrued wisdom; the confidence of having been there and got the T-shirt, as opposed to the uncertainties and neuroses of youth; the certainty that comes from dealing successfully with a lifetime of relationships and life-enhancing situations.

After all, people talk about 'the fountain of youth' – why don't we talk about the 'grey geyser' (not to be confused with 'grey geezer'!). Let's replace 'ageing' with 'sageing' and there is surely a fortune waiting for the person who produces a keep-fit video with the title 'Age without agues'. We must never regret growing old. Remember, the alternative is not that attractive, and the best age is the age you are. After all, age really doesn't matter unless you are a cheese or a wine – and both improve with age.

> 'Retirement at sixty-five is ridiculous. When I was 65, I still had pimples.'
>
> *George Burns*

What Is He?

by D. H. Lawrence

What is he?

–A man, of course.

Yes, but what does he do?

–He lives and is a man.

Oh, quite! But he must work. He must have a job of some sort.

–Why?

Because obviously he is not one of the leisured classes.

–I don't know. He has lots of leisure. And he makes quite beautiful chairs.

There you are then! He's a cabinet-maker.

–No, no!

Anyhow, a carpenter and joiner.

–Not at all.

But you said so.

–What did I say?

That he made chairs, and was a joiner and carpenter.

–I said he made chairs, but I did not say he was a carpenter.

All right then, he's just an amateur.

–Perhaps! Would you say the thrush was a professional flautist or just an amateur?

I'd say it was just a bird.

–And I say he is just a man.

All right! You always did quibble.

Don't Worry – Be Happy

When people are working, their life is strictly structured. They get up at the same time every working day. They follow a family routine of appointments in the bathroom and breakfast. They travel to work the same way each day, knowing how long it should take them by the minute.

At work, there are schedules, deadlines, meetings and the allocation of time is strictly monitored. Time means money and needs to be spent effectively. It is a major crime to waste it.

After work, it is the same predictable route home, followed by timetables for tea and other leisure activities. It has to be said, that most of these time constraints are imposed by other people. They are not self-imposed.

On the first day of retirement, that structure totally disappears. There is nobody to tell you how to spend your time, where you should be at a certain time and what you need to have achieved by a certain date.

This lack of structure does cause some people some problems.

Whilst you are at work, the 24 hours in each day is roughly split into three sections.

People normally spend eight hours sleeping, eight hours a day working and the other eight hours travelling, shopping or becoming involved in other leisure activities.

In life after work, the whole time allocation changes quite dramatically. No longer is a third of each day spent under the yoke of working. In addition, because people are not so stressed and exhausted from the daily grind, they need less sleep. They are more energetic and vigorous. They will probably only require about six hours sleep. This change leaves an enormous eighteen hours in every day for something like the next twenty years that needs to be filled – some 131,400 hours.

There is an enormous amount you can do in eighteen hours. You can fly from the UK to New York, have a leisurely dinner, take in a Broadway show, have a stroll round Times Square, have a good night cap and have a decent night's sleep in a hotel – and you can do this, or something similar, every day for the rest of your life.

Life Balance in Employment   **Life Balance in Retirement**

Sleep – Work – Leisure   Sleep – Work – Leisure

'To be able to fill leisure intelligently is the last product of civilization and at present very few people have reached this level.'

Bertrand Russell

It is this enormous availability of free time that poses some problems for some people.

At the time of their retirement they say that they have a number of jobs around the house that they need to do, and there is a lot in the garden to keep them occupied.

Filling the time in is not a problem. Becoming involved in activities that are satisfying and enriching is the real challenge.

And so, the attraction of this activity soon palls. There are only so many times you can decorate a room, or lay a patio. There is a finite limit to the amount of shelves you can put up. Working in the garden in the dark, dank days of winter is not all that attractive.

Released from the constraints of spending a third of your life earning a living, the possibilities of life after work are limitless. To get the best out of this opportunity, it would seem advisable to become involved in some sort of preparation and planning.

People who achieve the correct balance in their life do seem to achieve greater happiness, and in reality extend the length and quality of their lives.

This balance not only involves physical and mental health, but also emotional and spiritual well-being.

Happiness seems to be more than a feeling. It is a choice. It pays no attention to age, success, wealth or education. Circumstances do not cause an individual's happiness or unhappiness. It is determined by people's reaction to events.

Opinions vary, but it is generally accepted that there are eight elements involved in the achievement of this balance. It is useful to spend a little time examining these elements in some more depth. Read the following section, and give yourself a score out of ten for each of the eight elements.

The Wheel of Happiness

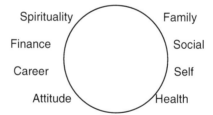

The Family

The first of these elements and one of the most important relates to the quality of family life. This is a good starting point on this journey into life after work. Just take a step back and examine the quality of your family life. Is your family more like the Simpsons or the Waltons? Does everybody get along well? Do they talk to each

More time with the family...

other? Are there any deep-seated differences of opinion between the various members of the family? On a scale of one to ten, how would you rate the quality of your own particular family life?

A harmonious and support family structure does seem to be a key element in this life balance – a family where everyone gets along well together (parents, brothers, sisters, sons and daughters, the extended family), where relationships are maintained and nurtured, where there are regular parties and social meetings, where there is a great deal of mutual support and affection.

At the other end of the spectrum is the family that is riven by feuds and family squabbles, where certain members of the family are ostracised and ignored.

There is constant bickering, lots of awkward silences and slamming of doors.

If your family is harmonious and supportive, give yourself a high score out of ten. If it is a constant cauldron of arguments and resentment, give yourself a lower score.

'The first half of our life is ruined by our parents and the second half by our children.'

Clarence Darrow

…and both are probably on drugs, anyway.

Social

The next significant element in any discussion about life balance is the area of relationships and social interaction. Many people report that one of the main aspects that they will miss about leaving work is their colleagues and friends and life after work is exactly the same.

You need a good, varied circle of stimulating friends, who you meet regularly to enjoy the richness of social occasions – a forum to share viewpoints and friendly debates about current affairs, different opinions and beliefs.

A good social circle is also a facility for meeting new people and for developing social intelligence, being interested in other people and their experiences, having an open mind, without being judgemental. This is particularly appropriate where the social circle includes younger people.

At the lower end of the 'social circle' spectrum is the person who prefers to be a social recluse – the person who avoids social contact like the plague, and ideally would prefer to be a crofter in the Outer Hebrides with neighbours ten miles away and in the company of a few quizzical sheep – somebody who is uncomfortable meeting new people and is not interested in improving social skills and broadening one's horizons.

Once again, give yourself a score out of ten. If you are a social person and have a good circle of friends, if you treat everybody the same and are genuinely interested in other people's viewpoints, then give yourself a high score.

If however you are an irritable curmudgeon, with the social skills of a hermit, preoccupied with your own opinions, then give yourself a lower score.

Self-esteem

The third significant element in the quest for a life balance is the notion of self-esteem.

There is no doubt that people who exhibit confidence in themselves and their own capabilities do adjust more successfully in the move into life after work.

Take a step back and consider this question. Are you comfortable with yourself as a person? Do you have a positive image of yourself? Do you love yourself, in the nicest possible way? When you look at yourself in the mirror, do you like what you see?

This has nothing to do with arrogance or cockiness, but involves a genuine positive acceptance of who you are. Confidence is not a commodity that can be bought or received as a gift from other people. It comes from within and is generated with a realistic appraisal of your own quality and ability.

Some people, for some reason, do have a low opinion of themselves. They indulge in bouts of false modesty. 'Oh, I could never do that', 'I am not like that', 'That's OK for other people but not for me', they repeat as a mantra.

It is the same in all walks of life and there is evidence to show that people who possess this inner strength and have a realistic appraisal of their own strengths and weaknesses are consistently more successful.

Where do you stand on the scale of confidence? If you feel good about yourself, and if you are a confident person, give yourself a high score out of ten. Ten out of ten might seem a little overconfident!

If you are a less confident person, and if you worry unduly about other people's opinions of you, then give yourself a lower score.

Health

The joker in the pack in all these considerations is the question of health and medical matters. Many people have a fatalistic approach to health issues, and by middle age you are probably not going to change the habits of a lifetime.

The issue here, however, is not about what illness or disease we are going to get, but about care and prevention.

The question is, do you look after yourself and take sensible measures that are generally recognised to reduce the onset of certain illnesses and medical conditions?

Do you eat a balanced diet? Do you drink in moderation? Do you take appropriate exercise? Do you treat your body as a Sikh temple or more like an Indian take-away?

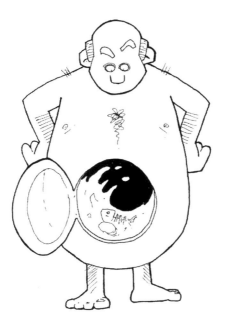

Do you treat your body as a Sikh temple,
or more like an Indian takeaway?

Health and medical issues are discussed later in the book, but for the purposes of the life balance exercise, a healthy existence is one of the main ingredients, and anything we can do to prolong and extend a healthy body and mind, we really should be doing.

How do you score on the health scale then? If you walk regularly, eat healthily, drink sensibly and perhaps exercise regularly, then give yourself a high score out of ten.

If you are a pie-guzzling, beer-swigging, couch potato, and are prepared to admit it, or if your idea of exercise is to switch the remote control from one hand to the other so that one arm doesn't become overdeveloped, then give yourself a somewhat lower score.

Attitude

Probably the most important aspect of the whole life balance question, attitude is the way people look at (and feel about) the outside world.

There are some people who do seem to live their entire life blaming other people and agencies for their current condition. They will blame their parents, their teachers, the boss, other colleagues, the computer, other departments, the government, even the weather. They say things like 'My parents never encouraged me', 'My teacher always said I was no good at Maths', 'It's all the Sales Departments fault.' They never seem to be in charge of their own destiny.

Their lives seem to be dominated by matters and people outside their control. The 'locus of control' resides outside, in the hands of other people.

These people are usually always extremely busy, and they never have time to listen to other people. They bemoan the old days and the previous ways of working and are usually quite arrogant in their own limited knowledge and experience, saying things like 'That'll never work', 'You don't want to be doing that, we've tried it before, it always fails.'

They waste most of their time and energy focused on the current situation and the attendant problems.

If you meet them in a corridor in a morning at the office and you say 'Good morning, how are you today?', they will go to great lengths to tell you about the death of their pet dog, the excruciating backache they suffer and even their wife's infidelity with the milkman.

Do you really want to hear this? You were only being polite.

Fortunately, there are other people in the world with a different attitude and approach to life. These people are rather pleasant people to be around. They do not blame other people or agencies for their current situation. They accept responsibility for it themselves. They squarely accept that they own the locus of control and they are solely in charge of their own destiny. They are busy people, but they can always make time for another person's observations. They are open-minded and keen to learn.

Above all they have a sense of perspective and demonstrate a keen sense of humour.

Approaching the transition away from work to a more independent existence, it is quite important that people do cultivate a positive mental attitude, if indeed they have not in the past.

Positive people will have approached each stage of their lives with this attitude.

Each significant event of their lives, starting school, passing examinations, getting the first job, getting married, bereavements, all will have been tackled and overcome with the energy and power of the positive approach. Research at the University of Texas seems to indicate that a positive attitude may even delay the ageing process.

Most of their time and energy is channelled into finding solutions to the problems.

So where do you stand with regard to your attitude. Is your glass half full or half empty? Some say, 'Who cares if your glass is half full or half empty, if your teeth are in it?' Do you always look on the bright side of life? Are you optimistic by nature?

If you are, mark yourself high on this scale of one to ten.

If you are, however, rather negative in outlook – if you can always see the problems rather than the solutions – then mark yourself lower.

Career

Assessing the value of career in your life balance may be difficult at this stage as you will be either leaving or contemplating leaving your current role as you are reading this. But we do need to examine your thoughts on your previous career. As we have seen, work plays a significant part in all our lives and for any balance to be achieved we do need to feel good about our time spent in pursuing career goals. Satisfaction at work is one of the most elusive of these goals.

How do you feel about your career? Do you feel positive about it? Do you feel you have made significant achievements? Has your potential be fulfilled? Have you been recognised and rewarded appropriately?

On the other hand, do you feel frustrated and undervalued? Do you feel alienated or bitter?

Give yourself a mark on the scale of one to ten to indicate how satisfied you feel about your working experience.

Money and financial matters

This is undoubtedly the most important aspect of life balance. It is difficult to achieve balance without feeling comfortable about your financial situation.

At this stage, however, we are not concerned with your bank balance or how many assets you own. Here we want to examine your approach and attitude to matters financial.

There are many millionaires who constantly worry about money and where the next buck is coming from. They feel financially insecure and are preoccupied with losing their fortunes.

Other people are head over heels in debt with loans and credit cards, yet seem to handle this situation with composure and equanimity.

The crucial question is, how do you approach and handle financial matters?

If you keep detailed financial records, if you carefully plan spending budgets, or if you don't open any bills that come through the door and throw unread bank statements into a draw, it is of no importance in this context. What really matters is how comfortable you are dealing with money and finance.

If you are comfortable with your own money regime, give yourself a high score out of ten.

If you are a worrier and wake up in a cold sweat during the night or jump when the telephone rings or when a knock comes to the door fearing the worst, then give yourself a lower score.

The final, but equally important element in the life balance spectrum is the notion of …

Spirituality and beliefs

The issue under consideration here is not whether you believe in God, whether you belong to any religion or are a regular churchgoer, but most specifically are you comfortable with the beliefs you hold, no matter what they are?

There are devout religious people who are wracked with self-doubt and uncertainty about their beliefs. There are atheists who are perfectly comfortable with holding these views.

As age progresses and one realises that one is no longer immortal, then more people do take interest in these matters. Are you comfortable with the ideas and beliefs that you subscribe to? Do you spend time worrying about whether there is a God or not? Do you consider what is the best way of worshipping that God?

Do you consider the question of life after death, why we are here, and what life is all about – and are you comfortable with your answers?

If you are comfortable with your beliefs then give yourself a high mark. If you are continually wracked with doubt and uncertainty give yourself a lower score.

As we can see, the concept of happiness is a complex one. If you ask people what will make them happy, some might say 'to win the lottery', or 'to lie on a beach in the Bahamas'. However, these are merely pipe dreams and even if they are achieved will probably not make or keep that person happy.

In reality, the concept of happiness does seem to embody some kind of balance of the eight elements listed above. Business or career success alone is no guarantee of happiness. You might meet a successful captain of industry who is almost off the scale when considering the success of his career and working life – but his family life is in tatters, his adolescent children are on drugs and his wife has moved in with her female fitness instructress.

There is no shortage of successful people in the professions who overly indulge with the grain and the grape, who are suffering from ulcers and other stress-related illnesses because they have not looked after their health.

This balance is now even more important as we approach the transition from work.

With the enormous amount of time now available to us, it does seem to be a realistic strategy to spend some of it improving and enhancing any or all of these elements.

Just revisit these areas now and concentrate on the areas where your score was in a lower category.

For example, if there is a problem within the family, we now have the time to sit down and discuss the problem in some detail with the interested parties. If a son has gone off the rails, or a daughter is mixing with the wrong company, what could be more beneficial than sitting down as a family and discussing the matter rationally? A solution may not be reached at the meeting but at least there is honest and concerned communication.

We now have the time to visit some estranged member of the family and we have the opportunity for more quality time with spouses and partners.

Another example may well be in the health element. We will now have more time to look after our bodies and improve our health regime, both physically and mentally.

Released from the permanent treadmill, many opportunities arise for physical exercise, leisure activities and programmes of self-development.

This balance will obviously change from time to time. Retirement is not some magical state where everything goes well and there are no problems and crises. It is exactly the same as any other stage of life, childhood, adolescence, and parenthood. The life balance will change from time to time. The key is first to be aware of the components of a happy and fulfilled life and then spend time enjoying the elements that are going well and working on the areas that need improvement.

Happiness is more than a feeling – it is a choice. It pays no attention to age, success, wealth, or education. Circumstances do not cause an individual's happiness or unhappiness. It is determined by people's reaction to events.

'It is not the strongest of the species that survives, not the most intelligent, but the one responsive to change.'
Charles Darwin

A picture paints a few words.

If you like to receive your information in a more visual form, you may want to do the following exercise.

EXERCISE

Draw a circle on a piece of paper.

Now divide the circle into eight segments.

Dissect each segment with just ten points, marking them one at the most central point and ten at the most peripheral point.

Now label each segment with the headings we have discussed above: Family, Social, Self-esteem, Health, Attitude, Career, Financial and Spiritual.

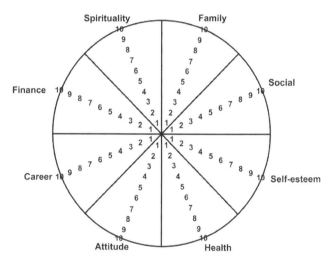

Give yourself a score out of ten for each segment and mark it by a cross on each scale of one to ten. You should then have eight crosses, one in each segment.

Next join up the each of these crosses, you will then come up with a configuration within the circle.

60

This is your 'Wheel of Happiness'. The rounder your configuration is, the smoother your passage through life should be; and the fuller the configuration is, for example if it shows nine's and ten's in each segment, the happier you will be.

For most people, however, this configuration shows a number of spikes, where each segment perhaps is not as perfect as it could be. The theory is that with all this extra time available to us, perhaps we should spend time and energy on these segments to improve them and achieve a rounder and fuller configuration.

If you do this exercise regularly, say every six months, you should begin to notice some change. Alternatively you may well lose the will to live and so there will no longer be a problem.

Measuring happiness

An innovative global measure of relative happiness, the Happy Plant Index, has been constructed by the New Economics Foundation and the Friends of the Earth. It uses three factors, life expectancy, human well-being and damage done via a country's 'environmental footprint'.

The country that is the happiest place on the planet is Vanuatu, formerly the New Hebrides, a South Pacific island nation. Vanuatu comes top because its people are satisfied with their lot, live to nearly 70 and do little damage to the planet. The big industrial nations fare badly. The United Kingdom trails in 108th place, below Libya, Gabon and Azerbaijan. The USA is 150th, and Russia is 172nd. Rather predictably Zimbabwe is at the bottom of the 178 nation list.

The Happy Planet Index essentially divides the damage we do environmentally by the payback through life expectancy and satisfaction. The survey seeks to convey that the environment damage being done by the wealthier nations, presumably in the pursuit of happiness and long life may have the opposite effect.

You can visit their website and compute your own Happiness Index based on these elements, but be prepared for some disappointment if you drive everywhere, never do any recycling and leave the light on all night.

Incidentally, we subsequently learned that in Vanuatu the courts were still trying people for cannibalism as late as 1996, so perhaps a fulsome diet was an important part of their happiness and longevity, and finger buffets were no doubt very popular.

In summary, we are not trying to explain 'Happiness'. As stated earlier, it is an enormously complicated subject. Life is difficult sometimes and it deals people some cruel blows.

However for the future perhaps every action you take should be judged against the following criteria. Will it raise my self-esteem? Will it give me emotional satisfaction?

Will it give me mental stimulation? Will it help me express my creativity? Does it have a sense of fun and adventure? Will it improve my physical fitness? Will it improve my social life?

If the answer to all of these is 'No', then don't do it. Go back to bed.

'Half of our life is spent trying to find something to do with the time we have rushed through life trying to save.'

Will Rogers

5

What are you going to DOOOO?

When you meet a newly retired person, they invariably report that they are extremely busy, busier even than when they were working. Whilst this in some cases may not be quite the case there is no doubt that people who keep active and have a range of interests and who become involved in a variety of activities certainly will enjoy a more fulfilling life after work. There is also evidence to show that these people actually live longer.

When surveys are conducted as to how they actually spend their time the results are rather revealing and the following is a list, by no means exhaustive, of activities in which they become involved.

More time with the family

As already outlined, family circumstances play a huge part in the pursuit of personal happiness. Retirement is not only a matter for the individual. It has a profound impact on the people around them, especially their spouses or partners.

If it is the man who is retiring, this has obvious implications for his wife. She has been used to her own routine around the house. She has her own priorities and commitments. She is the ruler of the household, and is in charge.

What can happen is that the husband with time on his hands seeks to change those priorities and alter these routines. He may want to usurp her authority in the running of the household, or may meekly follow her around the kitchen asking what needs to be done next.

It is profoundly ironic that it is during this period that they are forced to spend more time together than they have ever done previously. The children have probably grown up and left home. This new closeness can be a bonus or a burden. They may feel they have grown apart over the years and this new proximity proves to be rather uncomfortable. Strangely enough, one of the highest levels of divorce occurs in couples who are in this stage of their relationship.

There is the story of the couple in their eighties, who went to their lawyer seeking a divorce. When the lawyer asked them why they were considering divorce at this stage of their lives, they told him they had considered it much earlier but were waiting until the children had died.

Incidentally, John Mortimer likens divorce to one of those American cyclones – 'All that blowing and sucking early on, and you end up losing your house.'

However, returning to the positive aspect, with this newfound freedom couples can spend more time together and explore new avenues of closeness and companionability.

People want to spend time with their families for many different reasons. Some fathers suffer slight guilt feelings. Whilst the children were young and growing up, they were spending their time travelling or working long hours in the office or factory. They missed the wonderful years of being alongside their children as babies and toddlers.

They missed the quality time of the younger years and almost before they realized it, their children had grown up and become teenagers, ready to leave home and pursue their own lives independently.

These people are determined this is not going to happen again and they are determined to try and capture this period with their grandchildren. They arrange to spend more time with them, either as friends, playmates or unpaid babysitters.

Grandparents are infinitely more effective as babysitters. Not only are they free, but the parents know they won't raid the drinks cabinet or have it away with the boyfriend on the family couch.

There is no doubt that becoming an active and involved grandparent is a most enriching experience. To spend time with growing grandchildren is both rejuvenating and stimulating.

A great deal of perverse pleasure can be gained from this family activity. It is a great opportunity to embarrass your beloved offspring by recounting to the grandchildren some of the more bizarre episodes in the lives of their parents, when they were kids.

Tell them what they got up to – and gaily repeat some of these Kevin and Perry exploits that they were embroiled in so that when they are chastising their kids, the kids can always say, 'Well grandma, says that you always used to do it'.

Grandparents make great child minders…

It also a good opportunity for giving the grandchildren the most inappropriate of presents, and letting them indulge in behaviour that makes their parents apoplectic. Give them chocolates and ice cream, preferably before meal times. Let them make a mess of their rooms and play their music as loudly as they want. You could convince the little darlings that Christmas comes twice a year.

It can be payback time, particularly if the grandchildren are in their teenage years.

> 'You know you children are growing up when they stop asking where they come from and refuse to tell you where they are going.'
>
> *P. J. O'Rourke*

Some people use this extra time for healing family feuds and seek out estranged brothers and sisters. If there have been any longstanding family arguments and conflicts they reckon this is the time for forgiveness and reconciliation. They make contact with remote members of the extended family, with whom they have lost regular communication, and rekindle lost relationships.

How long did you say you'd been married to the miserable sod?

The Rest and Relaxers

These are the people, who consider they have spent enough time on the treadmill and all they want to do is put their feet up and relax. They want a quiet life, probably getting up a little later in the morning. They like to spend time doing household chores and pottering around in sheds and gardens. The emphasis is on relaxation and freedom from any stress.

They enjoy the soporific pleasure of listening to the afternoon play on the radio and anticipating the excitement of *The Archers* in the early evening.

According to viewing research figures, the average retired person watches television over 40 hours a week. This figure does not differ very much from the amount of time working people spend watching television and it is less time than younger people spend in front of their screens playing computer games.

The main point here is that they can do this without any feelings whatsoever of guilt.

They consider they have earned this position. They are freed from the pressures of organisational life and can enjoy the fruits of their labours. They take time to 'smell the coffee' and their motto is 'Why do today, what you can do tomorrow?'

> 'The time you enjoy wasting is not wasted time.'
>
> *Bertrand Russell*

The 'Good Timers'

These people approach retirement with a very positive outlook, in which all they want to do is enjoy themselves. They consider they have spent enough time in the rat race or on the treadmill and now they have earned their time in the sun.

They are hell-bent on enjoyment and seek out new, exciting experiences. They socialise more with friends in pubs and restaurants.

AHawieeee Five Oh!!

They host and attend more dinner parties with newer friends and acquaintances.

They try new cuisine, be it Vietnamese, Malaysian, Lebanese, and food from all over the world.

They attend the cinema and theatre more often and try new experiences like the opera and ballet. They go to jazz and pop concerts. They visit museums, art galleries, and other places of historical interest.

69

They take up amateur dramatics, join choirs, learn line and salsa dancing and any other social activity that appeals to the senses.

The Hobbyists

Even though they may not take up a new hobby, many people spend more time on the hobbies and pastimes they have always enjoyed. This encompasses a wide range of hobbies, pastimes, sports and other interests.

For the more active there is golf, walking, swimming, bowls, sailing, tennis, birdwatching and gardening. The more adventurous even extend to jet-skiing, abseiling, raft-building, archery and whitewater rafting. More sedentary pastimes include bridge, embroidery, stamp collecting, genealogy, book binding and collecting and model railways. Some people develop more expensive or esoteric hobbies such as vintage cars or the raising of exotic fish (the list is endless). Others take up a new musical instrument or brush up rusty skills on an old one abandoned some time ago.

Some develop their culinary skills and take great delight in conjuring up new and exotic meals. Some take up painting for the first time, or sculpture, or poetry. Ideally if the hobby can also involve some social interaction like bridge or some element of keeping fit like walking, so much the better. Fishing is the most popular sport in the UK.

For those people who, hitherto, have only been reading business reports and technical manuals, leisure reading can also become a popular pastime, including novels by good authors, autobiographies, crime and science fiction. The beauty of having read a popular novel is that you can always brag about it. Crosswords, word puzzles, and Sudoku are all good exercises for keeping the mind active. Good old train-spotting and even bus-spotting have their faithful adherents.

As an exercise, we surfed the internet for 'Hobbies' to see what would come up.

Whilst it is easy to scoff at other people's hobbies, we reproduce the list below without comment although some entries seem rather bizarre and would justify more enquiry.

Amateur & Ham Radio	Gardening	Railway Enthusiasts
Amateur Astronomy	Genealogy	Rockets
Aquariums	Handwriting Analysis	Gems and Minerals
Beachcombing	Home brewing	Scrap booking
Bell Ringing	Hula Hooping (?)	String Figures (?)
Birding	Jet Engines	Textiles
Books	Juggling	Tombstone Rubbing
Bubbles (?)	Kites	Treasure Hunting
Candle-Making	Knotting (?)	Urban Exploration
Cloud Watching	Lock picking (?)	Winemaking
Collecting	Magic	Wood Working
Crafts	Photography	Writing
Dolls	Pottery	
Electronics	Puppetry	
Games	Pyrotechnics	

We have queried a few rather strange pastimes, but with the range and scope of these activities, it does seem there is something for everyone and no need for anybody to be bored.

The Travellers

Currently, of course, many people are interested in travelling. Many are not just limited to sightseeing, but undertake educational trips, taking in local cultures.

With the advent of the internet and the cheap airlines, travel to the most exotic locations is becoming well within the reach of the average person.

If you are amongst those drawn to international travel, it may be a good idea to leave your name and telephone number with your local travel agent. Tell them your situation and your requirements so that they can contact you when any particularly good deals crop up. It is always useful to keep your passport handy and up to date.

Popular long haul destinations from the UK include Hong Kong, Vietnam, Laos, Thailand, Singapore, Australia, New Zealand, Fiji, South Africa, the Galapagos Islands, Peru, Brazil, Central America, the Caribbean, the USA, Canada, and Alaska.

Closer to home are Egypt, Greece, Cyprus, Sardinia, and the architectural delights and scenery of the ancient European cities. Old favourites like London, Paris and Rome are giving way to newer discoveries like Prague, Krakow, Budapest, Tallin and Valencia.

The cruise business is booming and many people give glowing reports of their cruising experiences. If you have ever been stuck in a traffic jam on any of Britain's A roads you will be aware how popular camping and caravanning are in Britain.

With the availability of air travel, many of the delights in Great Britain are overlooked.

The Highlands of Scotland, both Northern and Southern Ireland, Wales, the Lake District, the Yorkshire dales, Devon and Cornwall, the Fens, all hold great delights for the discerning traveller with time to spend. Really intrepid and seriously deranged travellers might sample the delights of Hull, or Hartlepool, or visit the Hat Museum and tour the underground air raid shelters in Stockport.

If you are that way inclined, you can visit the British Lawnmower Museum in Southport, or visit Eden Camp in Malton in North Yorkshire, which recreates WW2 living conditions in prisoner-of-war huts. The world is your winkle.

You need to be a little careful however, when travelling. A Yorkshire couple recently ended up with their car in the river. This was because the GPS system in their BMW failed to advise them to wait for a ferry.

Some travel philosophers advocate throwing away your Travel Guide Books. They maintain that once you read Guide Books, then you are seeing things through the eyes of the person who wrote the guide. This creates expectations, which are either met or fail to be satisfied.

Far better to see things through your own eyes and make your own decisions as to the relative beauty of the sight or if indeed it appeals to you personally.

In any case, as someone once said, it is the journey which is the most important part of travelling not the arrival.

It is the different sights you see on the journey, the interesting people you meet, the unplanned incidents that occur, these are the ingredients of successful enriching travel experiences.

Living Abroad

As an extension of this, many more people are deciding to up sticks and go and live abroad. Research shows that in less than ten years time, an extra 2.3 million people over 50 (one in eight) will be retiring abroad – and by 2020 one in five older Brits (an extra 4 million) will be living outside the UK. Popular destinations include France, Spain and America.

When asked what there motives were for moving abroad, the main answers were climate and environment, pace of life and health, lower living costs, and social advantages. The research also shows, not surprisingly, that people who have holidayed widely and tested the various locations available are those who will settle best when they finally do make the move.

It does require a certain type of individual and attitude for this move to be successful, however. One of the main prerequisites seems to be a passing familiarity with the local language. Those people who merely put an 'O' on the end of every word and gradually speak louder and louder to people who don't understand English, or say, 'Yes I can speak Spanish – Dos Cervezas', may find that perhaps living abroad is not for them.

A sensitivity to the local people is required – a curiosity about their history and culture, a flexibility when it comes to services and culinary requirements, a willingness to appreciate and absorb differences.

Most of all, it requires a sensible appreciation that there is no such thing as a 'dream' location; it is merely an alternative way of living and it has both its advantages and disadvantages.

Committee Men

Many retirees gravitate to involvement with committees. For them, being on a committee or on a community group is rather like a substitute for the working environment. There are regular meetings, agendas, minutes and action plans and in some ways it reminds them of work, particularly if they like clipboards and a row of pencils sticking out of their top pockets. They are using the skills that they were good at during their working life: administration, organisation and ability to get along with people. In fact these were often the people that made their work organization run smoothly and they now bring a sense of order and sense of purpose to any enterprise.

They become secretaries or treasurers at golf and sports clubs, and are the leading lights in any neighbourhood watch scheme or any community enterprise. They may develop political affiliations or consider becoming Justices of the Peace or school governors.

Volunteers and Charity Work

Many people become involved in a range of voluntary activities and charity work.

Often the motivation will be rooted in a sense that they are themselves rather fortunate. They are fit and well, and life has treated them rather kindly. They have probably spent the whole of their working life in an occupation which, although it has provided a livelihood for them and stability for their family, really has had little impact on the quality of life in the wider sense.

Their motivation is on a higher level. They feel that at this stage in their lives they want to 'put something back into society' or do something that 'really matters'. Hence, they volunteer to help and support sections of society who are not as comfortable or as able as they are themselves.

For some, the motivation is closer to home, when a member of their family or friends has suffered with a particular illness or ailment, as a result of which they wish to help other people in a similar position by fundraising or in other supportive roles.

Since the introduction of the National Lottery, registered charities have had to compete more professionally for resources. They desperately need the skills and knowledge of people with business experience.

Research has shown that people who volunteer their time, energy and expertise to a worthwhile cause, generally live fuller and longer lives. Charities and volunteer groups will beat a path to your door, once they know you are available. Helping older people by driving them to hospital appointments, assisting with Meals on Wheels, or generally providing pastoral support, or assisting in hospices and other institutions may not be everybody's cup of tea, but they are all deeply enriching and satisfying ways of spending your time.

Similarly, helping underprivileged children, young adults with problems, dysfunctional families and ex prisoners all are a positive way of putting something back into society.

If you have a sympathetic nature and enjoy helping people, consider using your skills to provide crisis counselling, legal advice or even companionship for the homebound and low-income groups. Youth-orientated community organizations welcome older volunteers, who have unique wisdom and patience.

The VSO organisation has recently raised its age level of entry to 65 indicating that this is not just an activity for young people, but they need people of relevant experience.

The Educationalists

For some people, especially those who missed out on higher or tertiary education, this is an ideal opportunity to catch up on their education. They spend this time in studying and self-development.

The activities range from taking a course at an evening class, learning a new language, or taking a course in Geography or Chemistry all the way through to taking a fully-fledged degree with the Open or any other university. A significant number of Open University degrees are awarded to mature students. Other popular interests are Astronomy, Architecture, and History of Art.

Nowadays, of course, the internet is a rich source for people seeking all forms of personal development. As well as learning online, people can exchange views and information by email, chat online, and even publish their own musings online in their own 'blogs'.

The University of the Third Age is a thriving ever expanding organization in the UK. It currently boasts some 155,000 members in over 500 branches. They offer a wide range of seminars, lectures and meetings ranging from the esoteric, to the fun, to the practical. It is also a great place to come into contact with like-minded people with similar interests.

Self-Employment

Some people become involved in setting up their own business, or buy an existing business. After spending many years imprisoned by bureaucracy and incompetence, they have always dreamed of running their own show. They are attracted by notions of time, freedom, romance and independence. They like the idea of being autonomous and becoming the decision-maker.

However, a word of warning for any readers who might have harboured dreams of running a small Post Office in the Lake

District, or a small pub in the Yorkshire Dales, or perhaps a Bed-and-Breakfast in Cornwall...

People with these notions really should be told to go and lie down in a dark room for a time, at least at the outset. In many instances, these aspirations really are no more than pipe-dreams. Establishing a business is an extremely hard undertaking.

The danger is that one set of bosses is just replaced by another set, consisting of bank managers, the VAT people, the Inland Revenue and a motley crew of customers and clients. It is not a part-time enterprise, and people who run their own business will tell you that it is a twenty-four hours operation.

One in three new businesses fail in the first year and three out of five do not last more than five years.

However, given all this, some talented people do make a great success of setting up their own business. These are the people who seek advice prior to setting up, and do not rush into it without considering the reality of their project. They have clear plans and business goals. They have good health. When you are on your own, there is no opportunity to phone up on a Monday morning complaining of a virus or a tummy bug. They are 'jacks of all trades', and they are prepared to get stuck into a whole range of activities. There is no room for prima donnas in this business.

These successful people are action people. They are not hampered by too much deliberation and paralysis of thought. They are certainly not 'Gunners' – people who are always 'gunna' do this or 'gunna' do that. They just go out and do it.

They are comfortable with making difficult decisions and whilst they are not gamblers, they are happy to take calculated risks. One important aspect of successful businessmen is that they do not have any fear of failure. They are prepared for failure as long as they learn something from that failure. Most successful people have not become successful immediately, but have undergone a series of painful failures before hitting the right note.

But most of all, these successful people are immensely resilient and persistent. They know what they want and nothing deters them from achieving it. Being in your own business is akin to living on a roller coaster. The joys and rewards when the business is thriving are unimaginable to the uninitiated. To think that success has been achieved off one's own bat is a most euphoric and edifying experience. The highs are immensely high.

But it is the dark times that really separate the winners from the losers. This is where these successful people display enormous reservoirs of resistance and reserves of inner strength.

If you feel you possess these qualities, if you have a great business idea, if you have sought advice from professionals, if you have a realistic business plan and you are clear what you want from the business, then by all means go ahead with it, because you might always regret that you didn't do it when you had the chance.

Franchising

Increasing numbers of people are attracted by the idea of buying a franchise to an established brand or business. They consider it to be a half way house between the risk of running one's own business and the security of being associated with an established business programme.

No doubt, some of these ventures are extremely successful but before making any decision there are serious considerations about the initial fee, any monthly commissions or charges, the freedom to operate within the business framework and any training that is available. After all, there is no such thing as a free lunch and this form of trading is just as vulnerable as any fledgling business.

Part-Time Work

A good number of retirees become involved in part-time paid work. The motivation here is that they want a small income just to top up their pensions.

Today with the fragmentation of the work place, with initiatives like job-share, maternity and paternity leave, flexitime and with the growing emphasis of the Work/Life Balance, there have never been more opportunities for part-time working.

Many small to medium-sized companies can benefit from the skills and experience gained from a lifetime working in a large organisation.

Full-Time Work

Strangely enough, a number of people seek out full-time employment. Hopefully they do not jump from the frying pan into the fire but this time around they choose something that they really enjoy doing.

Some dedicated people go through the process of submitting CVs and application forms. They are prepared to undergo the indignity of the selection interview, where they are questioned by Human Resource clones with two years experience after obtaining a degree in Origami or Media Studies at a former polytechnic somewhere near Scunthorpe.

It is at this stage that the 'A' word surfaces. Ageism is practised among consenting adults throughout British commerce and industry. But it is almost impossible to get anybody to admit to it. Human Resource people, whatever that means, seem to have the mistaken view that it is their role in life to keep people out of the company. They maintain a wall of silence and mock protestations.

There are plans to make discrimination on grounds of age illegal. This, like any legislation, will merely change the battleground. Practitioners will become even more devious and elusive.

Fortunately the climate is changing, mainly driven by basic economics and value for money. Organisations are becoming weary of the lack of commitment and dedication of some young people. Many suffer from stratospheric absenteeism figures, especially on Monday mornings. What could be termed the old-fashioned virtues of reliability, integrity and loyalty are now re-emerging and are being valued once again. The myth that older people are harder to train and slower to learn should have been dead and buried long ago. There are many seventy-year-olds with more energy and enthusiasm in their little fingers than some teenagers can boast in their entire bodies.

Shelf-stacking at a local superstore is no longer the only option. Mature workers bring a lot to the party. Most are dedicated and committed work colleagues. They usually rub along well with other people. Rather than being resistant to change, many of them have spent their whole working lives at the forefront of change. They have been in organisations that have adapted to the changes in technology.

They have managed re-organisations and restructurings. They have experienced the effects of globalisation and the changing nature of customer demands.

There are many people now who pursue what is called 'portfolio' careers, which entails having a range of interests and moneymaking activities. Many also put their skills and experience to good use as consultants or interim managers.

Perhaps, now that finance is not the main issue, people can choose to become involved in a role which they really enjoy. There is a whole range of opportunities both in the private and the public sectors. For those that want it, there is ample chance for a second career.

In their excellent book *You...Unlimited,* Messrs McCrudden, Bourne and Lyons give some excellent advice on living the portfolio life. They build on the original concept of Charles Handy's in his book *The Age of Unreason.*

Handy explains his concept as ' ....a portfolio of activities – some we do for money, some for interest, some for pleasure, some for a cause .... the different bits fit together to form a whole greater than the parts.'

You...Unlimited is a step-by-step practical guide to planning and translating this concept into reality. As the structure of organisations has become flatter and layers of management have been stripped out, there has been an explosion in outsourcing and contracted work. Many people have seized the opportunity to take early retirement and embark on careers as consultants and interim managers.

The American Dream

It is always difficult to get first-hand knowledge of how retirees spend their time, but in 2002 a survey was carried out by Harris Interactive in the United States.

The results are interesting and show that people's expectations during retirement have changed dramatically.

Less than a quarter of people over 55 – including retirees and pre-retirees – see their retirement as mainly a 'winding down'. Most see retirement either as a continuation of their life before retirement or as the start of a whole new life.

The overwhelming majority (95%) of those not retired who were planning to retire, expected to do at least some work after retirement. Those aged 55 to 64 wanted to continue to learn (81%), to try new things (70%), to travel (65%) (a particularly high score for the average American), and to have a new hobby or interest (63%).

Based on a detailed analysis of the results, it was able to divide those over 55 into four groups, depending on their hopes and expectations.

"Ageless Explorers" (27%)

This group personifies the new deal for retirement. Not satisfied with traditional norms of retirement, they seek to be active and independent in retirement. They would rather be too busy than risk being bored. Taking advantage of their good health and, for many, the companionship of their spouses, they want to live life to the fullest, participating in numerous recreational, leisure and personal growth activities. They desire personal freedom and flexibility in order to make the most of this stage of their life.

Ageless Explorers have the resources to achieve their goals as they have made nearly all the right moves in preparing for retirement. They are well educated, and have earned and invested significant amounts of money. They have received investment advice and developed an overall investment strategy to achieve financial independence in retirement. Being sound of body, and with an active spirit and solid finances, Ageless Explorers see retirement as a continuance of what life has been.

"Comfortable Contents" (19%)

This group seeks a more traditional view of retirement. While they enjoy travel and recreational activities, they are content to relax and enjoy the fruits of their labour.

This is fulfilment for them. They are feeling perfectly happy with life as it is today. They are less willing than other segments to risk feeling stressed in retirement. They have worked to achieve their happiness by saving and investing well and by having an overall financial strategy.

Work in retirement is not of interest to Comfortable Contents – they've done that. They are also the least likely to feel a need to contribute to society. Instead, they are enjoying the rewards of good health and good financial planning through relaxation and play – living their golden years.

"Live for Todays" (22%)

This group aspires to many of the same new retirement ideals laid out by the Ageless Explorers, and they may be even more interested in personal growth and reinvention. They dream to have time to do the things they haven't had time for earlier in life, including spending time on hobbies, travelling and community affairs.

'Live for Todays' see themselves as adventuresome and exciting. For them, retirement represents the opportunity for a whole new life, and possibly a transformation.

However, most 'Live for Todays' have been so focused on the 'here and now' during their working years that they did not build a financial base for their retirement years. They are not as nearly financially well off as either Ageless Explorers or Comfortably Contents, and are worried that they will not have enough money saved for retirement.

Sick and Tireds (32%)

This group is living the worst possible scenario for retirement. They are less educated and have fewer financial resources than the other retirees and a significant portion of this segment are likely to be widowed and in poor health.

They are less likely to travel, visit family, participate in community events or tap into their human potential. They are just trying to hang on, having faith that strong religious beliefs are the key to living a long life.

This group is likely to view their retirement years as a winding down of their lives.

And so, retirement seems different things for different people. Historically, we have lived a linear life plan. You were born, you grew up, you got married, you had children and then you died.

In the 21st century, we may well have a cyclical life plan. For the future, people may well go back to school on a number of occasions, they may well get divorced and fall in love again. They may well have years away from work, in which to enjoy their lives and not leave it until the end of their career working life.

'Old age is the most unexpected thing ever to happen to man.'

Trotsky

To complete this chapter, have a go at the exercise set out overleaf.

Ten things I have always wanted to do but I have never had the time.

    1.

    2

    3

    4

    5

    6

    7

    8

    9

    10.

Perceived barriers preventing me from achieving these goals.

    1.

    2

    3

    4

Real barriers preventing me from achieving these goals.

    1   Me

6

The Joker in the Pack

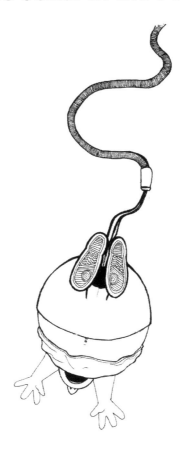

'If I'd known I was going to live this long, I'd have taken better care of myself.'

Eubie Blake, Jazz Musician, on 100th birthday

The *Which Guide to an Active Retirement* devotes thirty-two pages to health, listing all diseases from arthritis to varicose veins that older people are prone to and likely to contract. Many of these diseases, however, are just as likely to be contracted by younger people, and it gives a false perception of the healthy life that many mature people enjoy. Incidentally, there is a noticeable absence of any advice about sexually transmitted diseases.

Let's look at health in a bit more detail. Most people associate retirement with aches, pains, loss of mobility, and so on. Whilst it is true that for most of us there is some deterioration in our physical well-being, we have got to put this into a proper perspective once we contemplate retirement. We need to be aware of our physical condition and develop a healthy regime to suit our own personal needs.

Of course we can't run the mile in four minutes, but could we ever? What we have to do is to sort out the importance of distinguishing our mental from physical health. Science tells us that our brains don't really slow down. OK, we're losing brain cells, but we've still got a huge chunk left, so we don't need to bother about that. Our own experience and discussions with elderly relatives tells us that old age does not diminish our enthusiasm for things that interest us, like sport or gardening or even sex. So we have to continue with these interests and maybe develop others, if they appeal. In any event we have got to keep the old brain ticking over. Remember the quotation 'a healthy body needs a healthy mind' – was it the Ancient Greeks or the Duke of Edinburgh who said that? Well it doesn't matter, really, since they are probably one and the same.

So when we retire we have got to give some thought to continuing with existing interests and developing new ones. Remember, don't feel inhibited in any way. If you fancy becoming the conductor of an orchestra or an aircraft pilot or even a brain surgeon – give it a go. If it's something you've always wanted to do, a wish unfulfilled – even better. Do not be put off by well-meaning idiots who think they know better.

Think of all those old people who have taken up marathon running or parachuted out of an aircraft in their eighties – give it a go.

Which brings us to the importance of physical health.

This we can divide between exercise and diet, both tricky subjects if we are to believe the various theories on offer.

Turning first to exercise…

Now this issue is going to be down to each individual.

If you have never been particularly active during your life, then going berserk on retirement might well cause a problem. You may not want to embark on a new life surrounded by trainers and gyms.

There are two solutions.

The first is to rely on your genes to see you through. You've heard the stories where the individual claims his father lived to be ninety and smoked and drank all his life. This approach may work, if you are lucky or if your genes really are able to keep you going, but for the majority of us this approach is not going to do the trick.

After all, one of your objectives is to live as long and as happily as possible, drawing your pension for as long as possible, to the consternation of the organisation and the state.

This brings us to the second solution: exercise.

For most of us, some sort of exercise seems to be the order of the day – but how much? There are no easy answers. It is going to depend on what you are comfortable with. For some, an hour every day in the gym will be fine. For others, walking in the country will do equally well.

Don't forget that the experts say that a brisk walk for half an hour each day is all that most of us need to keep in reasonable shape.

If even that is too much, regular sex may help. After all, it amounts to about 200 calories a time, so even this may offer a solution.

In the main, the important thing is that whatever exercise you choose, it should be regular, in moderation, and it should be sufficient to keep the system ticking over.

Diet is another factor, which causes most of us to look the other way, and why not since when you come to retirement there should be some relaxation from the iron regimes of business lunches and high-powered expense accounts – if you're lucky.

The problem today is that we are faced with a huge variety of advice, much of which appears contradictory. Before modern medical advances the advice was straightforward – namely, that we should avoid fatty foods and eat more greens. But over recent times the picture has become less clear-cut.

For example, alcohol is bad, but not red wine; butter should be avoided – well, perhaps not; chocolate, like all sweet things, is forbidden, but not dark chocolate; carbohydrates should be reduced, but maybe not, and so the problems multiply.

Keeping up with the changes in dietary rules has become a full-time occupation, and not one for retirees. Leave that to the young and anxious, who want to live to be two hundred.

However as part of our programme to remain fit and happy, some thought has to be given to this problem.

Firstly we should try and avoid putting on weight, but this requires some sort of target weight that we are comfortable with. Most of us are sensible people and whilst we may occasionally remind ourselves of the slim outlines of the past, common sense dictates that this will stay in the past. So we have to decide are we comfortable with our present size. If the answer is 'yes', fine, so long as we are being honest with ourselves. Twenty-six stone and five feet six inches tall is not being as honest as twenty-six stone and seven foot six.

If weight needs to be lost, find a comfortable way of losing weight, without going into a depression, and if it takes six months to lose half a stone, so what? Once the target weight has been achieved, relax and get on with life, but remember to try and maintain it.

With regard to dietary habits, the only advice which seems sensible is to eat most things, including greens, in moderation and the only time to worry about your weight is when you stand on a talking weighing machine and it says 'One at a time, please.'

We move on now to the sensitive issue of smoking.

Most of us have been smokers and some of us have managed to give it up. But what about those who haven't? Most of the evidence seems to indicate that smoking is bad for us, but if you are a smoker is this much help? It's an addiction and not easy to overcome, so if you can stop smoking, all to the good. There are now many programmes run by the NHS and local clinics to assist, so give it a try and see how you get on. You never know, you might even save money for the next holiday.

> 'The only way to keep your health is to eat what you don't want, drink what you don't like and do what you would rather not.'
>
> *Mark Twain*

Another area where the health police are at their most vehement is alcohol consumption. There is no shortage of medical experts and consultants to the Temperance Society, all spouting dire warnings about the dangers of consuming too much alcohol.

Whilst never decrying the misery of those poor people addicted to a bottle of vodka before breakfast, or the profound detrimental effects it can have on people's lives and relationships, a balanced approach to drinking has never hurt anybody. If people feel that having a couple of drinks gives them confidence or it makes them more attractive, so what?

As they say, 'Beer has helped ugly people make love for many years.'

> 'The only reason, I would take up jogging is so I could hear heavy breathing again.'
>
> *Erma Bombeck*

Attitudes to health and exercise have been turned on their head recently by two German health scientists Dr Peter Axt and Dr Michaela Axt-Gadermann.

In their book, *The Joy of Laziness*, they provide a very attractive proposition. They maintain that every body has a certain amount of 'life energy', and that people who conserve their life energy live longer and fitter lives than people who expend their energy on meaningless, strenuous exercise.

People who lie in longer are apparently more effective than people who leap out of bed at the crack of dawn and the authors argue that an indolent, lazy life style is at the heart of good health. They point out that the longest living animal is the turtle, not an animal known for its exercising capacity and animals that hibernate live longer than animals that don't.

They are both former champion athletes, and based on scientific research they make the following claims;

- Too much exercise can make you ill
- Being relaxed and even-tempered makes you more intelligent
- Fasting delays the ageing process and lengthens your life
- Sun and heat are fountains of youth
- 'Doing nothing' actually does a great deal of good.

This is a particularly enticing point of view.

As with most of these studies, the research has been conducted on the poor laboratory mouse and so needs to be treated with some healthy scepticism. Another gentleman who pursues the same method is Cambridge University geneticist, Aubrey de Grey, who believes that life expectancy in humans could reach 1000 years in the not-too-distant future. He claims that ageing is a physical phenomenon happening to our bodies, so at some point in the future, as medicine becomes more and more powerful, we will inevitably be able to address ageing, just as effectively as we address many diseases to day.

He is the Director of the SENS (Strategies for Engineered Negligible Senescence) project to prevent and cure ageing. It is not just an idea, but a detailed plan to repair all types of molecular and cellular damage that happen to us over time. This is not just some science fiction creation but he reckons that the first person to live to 1000 might be 60 already.

All heady stuff. The fact that Dr de Grey also runs the Methuselah Mouse prize for extending age in mice could either enhance his credibility or diminish it depending on your point of view.

One aspect of growing older is possible need for medical care and health support. One place that you do not want to be these days, if you are ill, is anywhere near a hospital. All the research on longevity shows that people with minimal contact with the medical system live longer. You have been warned.

If you do have to go into hospital, you must be wary of any attempt to perform 'keyhole' surgery on you. If you have to have somebody operate on you, you at least want them in the same room. Operating through the keyhole seems to make the whole process too complicated and is the height of occupational arrogance and self-indulgence.

If you are like George Bernard Shaw and every time you think of doing some exercise you go and lie down until it wears off, then the thought of joining your local 'Health Club' may be anathema. Some people, however, bite the bullet and give it a go. When you visit these temples to sado-masochism, if you can get past the supercilious receptionist and the patronizing personal trainer, and master the intricacies of the exercise appliances which are the modern equivalent of medieval torture machines, then the whole process may be beneficial in some way.

One problem here is that you may have to reconsider fashion and evaluate the attire that you wear for doing exercises currently. The string vest and baggy shorts, held up with an old tie round the waist, black woollen socks and brown sandals may not cut any ice in today's fashion-conscious health clubs and gymnasia.

Some tight-fitting, body hugging, slinky number in Lycra may attract admiring glances and you never know, some of them may be from women.

Make an impression at your local Health Club...

A topic, which has almost become a taboo is the topic of sex involving mature people.

It does conjure up some images, that fall short somewhat of the ultimate epitome of grace and beauty, but this activity still plays a big part in the health and well-being of the mature person. Mature people have two distinct gifts in this area: time and experience. It is a case of Calmer Sutra.

'I delight in men over seventy, They always offer one the devotion of a lifetime'

A Woman of No Importance, Oscar Wilde

97

All the advice from 'relationship' experts is that: 'You should use it…or lose it.' (Perhaps more appropriate for some mature males, especially in the cold weather, should be: 'First find it… then use it or lose it.') But note that contrary to popular belief the term 'sexagenarian' has nothing to do with sexual appetite.

Any activity that you have performed thousands of times will lose its freshness and mystery. Some males report that it is like 'playing snooker with a rope'. They say they are at the age when they cannot take 'Yes' for an answer, and they become quite proficient at feigning headaches and other immobilising complaints. They are at the stage when 'getting lucky' means they can find their car in the car park.

'It's so long since I've had sex, I've forgotten who gets tied up.'

Joan Rivers

What must be remembered is that a male's interest in sex peaks in his early twenties and then declines steadily over the rest of his life. On the other hand, female interest does not peak quite as high or as early, but remains relatively constant over a much longer period. In later years, the menopause clearly has an effect, but any lack of interest (or ability) is more likely to fall on the male side than the female. This difference in interest level needs sensitive consideration!

All the advice is that in a loving relationship anything goes. Experimentation, role-playing, dressing up in uniforms, use of toys and other equipment, different locations and positions. Having said this, though, nobody in his right mind could find a Chelsea shirt erotic, could they?

The strategic use of pills, pumps and puppets may be a bit excessive, but you can still swing from the chandeliers or jump off the top of the wardrobe. Even missionaries must occasionally use different positions. Who cares? As long as it doesn't frighten the horses and both parties are comfortable and reach a level of satisfaction. For some 'Safe Sex' may mean having an oxygen tent, nitroglycerin pills and a blood pressure monitor by the side of the bed.

In a recent survey, three out of four women said they preferred gardening to sex. This presumably is because when gardening, they can move their own earth.

Dr Ruth Brewer in her eminently readable book *Intimate Relations* makes the following valid point:

'Research shows that men who are more sexually active actually live longer. Hormones are released during sex...men who have sex twice a week live longer than those who have sex once a month or less. In women it can fight the effects of menopause and reduce wrinkling.'

We have left a space above for you to fill in your own jokes based on this information. For those who are now wondering if they will make it to their next birthday, please be consoled that it must be a knockout chat up line... 'I can help you reduce your wrinkles...'

Perhaps a final word on the subject: a recent newspaper article highlighted the fact that more money is being spent into research on drugs like Viagra than the money being spent on researching a cure for Alzheimer's Disease, a truly sad state of affairs. By the year 2030 there will be crowds of older men wandering around with great erections and absolutely no recollection of what to do with them.

> 'The things that stop you having sex as you get older are exactly the same as those which stop you riding a bicycle – bad health, thinking it looks silly, no bicycle.'
>
> *Alex Comfort*

As a role model we are strongly attracted to the reports of the lifestyle of our late lamented Queen Mother. She was by all accounts no stranger to the delights of Bacchus. Former equerry Major Colin Burgess claimed in his book *Behind Palace Doors* that she had been known to start at noon with her favourite tipple, gin and Dubonnet, then to lunch with red wine followed with port, followed by a couple of martinis at six and champagne and claret for dinner. Whatever the truth of this, it is clear that she lived her life to the full. Now that is one helluva feisty woman.

Good on yer, Bess!

The search for longevity

An article in the National Geographic, November 2005, described the findings of researchers who had fanned out across the globe to find the secrets of long life.

Funded in part by the US National Institute on Ageing, scientists have focused on several regions where people live significantly longer.

In Sardinia, one team of demographers found a hot spot of longevity in mountain villages where men reach 100 with an amazing frequency.

On the islands of Okinawa, Japan, another team examined a group that is the longest-lived in the world.

And in Loma Linda, California, researchers studied a group of Seventh-day Adventists who rank among America's longevity all-stars.

Residents of these three places produce a high rate of centenarians, suffer from a fraction of the diseases that commonly kill people in other parts of the developed world and enjoy more healthy years of life.

So what is the formula for success? I hear you crying out.

To summarise, briefly...

In Sardinia, the locals drink red wine in moderation, couples share the sometimes arduous rural workload, and their diet includes pecorino cheese and other omega-3 foods.

The Okinawans maintain life-long friendships, eat small portions and find a purpose in life, be it yoga or fishing or some other focused activity.

The Adventists are teetotal, drink five pints of water a day, eat nuts and beans, observe the Sabbath and have a strong faith. I can already hear the cynics among you saying that people living in this community might not be actually living longer; it just *seems* such a long time.

Perhaps what is more important, however, is the common thread that runs through all these societies. They all put family first; they are all physically active every day; they keep socially involved; and their diet includes a lot of fruits, vegetables and whole grains.

So they offer a series of 'best practices'. It may be a bit impracticable to up sticks and horn in on these societies at this stage of your life, but the rest is up to you.

One observation the author Dan Buettner did make, however, was that in all the people he interviewed, 'there was not one grump in the bunch.' Perhaps conviviality is the secret to longevity. Perhaps you can start your own quest for longevity by easing up on the grump quotient. You and everyone else around you might just live longer.

Whilst it is encouraging that life expectancy is increasing all the time, nobody really wants to live longer if it is a case of putting up with a variety of age-induced illnesses and diseases.

Research into age-related illnesses was non-existent before the 1990's because it was felt that nothing could be done about it. There is now a substantial body of evidence, particularly in America, that health expectancy will at least keep pace with or even overtake life expectancy. Through improved healthcare and better education on health risks, people will be living longer but they will also spend these extra years in a better state of health.

"Look at that Paula Radcliffe – knackered after fifteen miles – what a disgrace"

7

The Root of Evil
(for Other People)

Letter to the Times. Sept 22 1988

Sir, I recently dined out at a pretentious hotel. When presented with an exorbitantly high bill for an indifferent meal, I drew the waiter's attention to a prominent notice, which offered 'special reductions for old age pensioners'. 'That, Sir,' he explained disdainfully, 'relates not to our charges, but to the size of the portions.' You have been warned.

Yours etc. Dr Allan H. Briggs.

Financial worries seem to be the main concern of those about to retire. This is understandable in that suddenly having to adjust from a regular monthly salary to something which is half that amount, or less, is never going to be easy. But wait, what about the lump sum, which can also be expected? This can amount to two or three times the salary, and seems to lighten the shadow, which may have fallen.

In practice most of the people who have retired recently in the UK, or who are about to retire, are individuals who have contributed to a final salary scheme. Our generation maybe the last to benefit from such generosity, since it would seem that our children might not look forward to such benefits. So we need to make the most of it while we can.

As previously mentioned, our attitude towards money will colour the decisions taken as to how to invest the lump sum. The most cautious amongst us would want to keep it under the mattress for safekeeping. This used to be a lot easier when we had paper pound notes. Now that we have £1 coins, the mattress gets a bit lumpy.

Well that's certainly an option, although in truth it is probably not the best one. Apart from anything else, it obviously fails to take into account the serious problem of inflation. Although the days of 15% inflation a year are hopefully a thing of the past, not to return, there is still an average of between 2 and 4% a year to consider, depending on which inflation index you use. If you have, say, £50,000 under the mattress that's a fair amount of money you are losing each year – the equivalent of £2,000 at 4% on an annual basis. So something needs to be done to address this problem.

One way is to reduce your overheads and pay off your mortgage. Since most of us are asset-rich in terms of the value of our homes this is not a bad idea. What this might allow you to do is sell your home, move into something smaller, pocket the difference and go on more holidays. If you've already paid off the mortgage or you still have extra cash left over from the lump sum and you are fed up with extra holidays the problem now is what to do with this money.

How to tackle this will depend on how comfortable you are with risking your money.

If you want to sleep at night without worrying about losing the lot then you need to invest it as safely as you can. If you are prepared to take a chance then the rewards maybe higher – it is up to you. In practice we can all find ourselves somewhere on a slope, which goes from minimum risk to 'the sky's the limit'.

The experts suggest that minimum risk entails investing in government bonds or gilts or perhaps with National Savings products. The rationale is that if the government goes bust, then we'll all in the mire, anyway. The returns on these investments are reasonable, but not fantastic, but they are safe. If you're feeling a bit more adventurous, banks and building societies offer bonds and various accounts, which will give you a better return. There is a slightly higher risk with these, since the bank or building society could conceivably go to the wall, but it is worth a chance. After this you move up the risk scale into the stock market with stocks and shares. At this point you will generally get a much higher return, but you have to accept a much higher risk.

There is a compromise position, which you can adopt. This entails adopting another suggestion from the experts. Why not divide your money into three equal portions: the first you invest in government or National Savings products; the second into banks or building society products; and the third you use to have a punt on the stock market. By using your money in this way you are helping to minimise risk and at the same time taking advantage of increased investment potential.

Another useful suggestion is to have a reserve cash fund set aside for emergencies.

You never know, one of your children might decide to get married for the fifth time, saying that they love wedding cake, and you might need some money to fund a new outfit, or what about changing the car, or even worse the roof needs re-tiling... In any event, keep a small sum of cash on one side for the rainy day, which we hope never comes, but almost always does.

Another way to invest the money is to buy property. The idea of buying a house, renovating it and then letting it out seems, on the surface, very attractive. No doubt there are some people who make a reasonable income from this enterprise and with house prices seemingly on an unending upward spiral, the prospect of long-term capital gains is infinitely attractive.

There are, however, numerous pitfalls. Maintenance costs, particularly on older type property, can be prohibitive. There are also barren periods, when the property is not let and sadly some tenants are extremely reluctant to pay promptly or to keep the property in a reasonable state.

> 'I have a deep conviction that all money not spent on good wines and spirits, fine cigars and tobaccos is just money wasted.'

> *J. B. Priestley*

There will be an army of people beating a path to your front door, wanting to separate you from your lump sums. One of the difficulties is deciding which source of information you can trust. Banks, insurance companies and other financial institutions will all have vested interests, and as a result may well be biased in their advice. You have only to witness the enormous profits posted by these institutions over the last few years to see just how successful they are in doing what they do.

Hence the introduction of the 'Independent Financial Advisor' (IFA) which in many cases is a bit of a contradiction in terms. However there are advisors out there who are genuinely professional and unbiased in the advice they give.

"My wife had her credit cards stolen but we haven't notified the police because the thief is spending it slower than she can."

We all know there is no such thing as a free lunch, and anybody who says they will double your investment in three years without any risk should come with a health warning. Here's an illustration of the kind of advisor you should definitely avoid.

They will probably turn up at your door in a BMW, wearing an Armani suit; they may wear a Homer Simpson tie to indicate that they have personality; and they will immediately start calling you by your first name as though they have known you for years.

They will probably be well versed in all aspects of selling techniques and will unashamedly base their pitch on feelings and emotions. Particularly they will play the eternal fear of ending up as a cabbage in a nursing home with no finances to support you.

They will tell you what you need rather than find out what you want. You should politely show these people the door and make a mental note to tell all your friends about this company.

The first thing a professional advisor will do is to ask you to sit down and look at your current finances and complete a Budget Planner (see page 112 for an example), projected into your retirement years.

This should be the basis for any initial discussion.

They will then ask questions and listen carefully to your answers. What are your plans, what are your dreams and what is your attitude to risk and income?

It may be best to choose a small to medium sized-company where you will get personal service and where the company has a range of people with different experiences and expertise.

You should look for an advisor who is thorough, consistent, interested and efficient.

Somebody who understands your needs, who does not blind you with jargon – ultimately, someone you can trust. Any advice they give you should be tailor-made to your needs and not off-the-shelf products.

In all this consideration of finance and money, we must never confuse a high standard of living with quality of life. There are many people with quite limited incomes who enjoy fulfilling and exciting lives.

One thing you may want to do is find out how much money you are entitled to under the Government Pension Scheme. As a rule of thumb, if you have worked and made your National Insurance contributions for 44 years then you are entitled to a maximum pension of something like £80 per week. Hardly a sum that will keep you in your champagne lifestyle, but money that is available, and it is better off in your pockets, rather than the government's. There is a form BR 19, which you complete and send to the Pensions Service in Newcastle and they will give you a pensions forecast.

Other legal considerations are that you really should make a will to avoid a messy situation after your demise and you may want to make plans to mitigate the effects of Inheritance Tax.

The other alternative is to go out and spend it all frivolously and with great abandon.

A good way to worry your kids is to let them know you are in the process of making a will and then leave brochures for cats' and dogs' homes around the house for them to pick up. Why not be a financial burden to your kids? They were a burden to you. Leave the EKI club (earning the kids' inheritance) and join the SKI Club to *spend* the kid's inheritance. It might be better to leave them all with a substantial debt, which they have to pay off. If you do this, they will certainly remember you longer.

'One good thing about being poor is that when you are 70, your children will not have declared you legally insane in order to gain control of your estate.'

Woody Allen

BUDGET PLANNER

HOUSE & HOUSEKEEPING	Current	In Retirement	RECREATION & PERSONAL	Current	In Retirement
Council Tax			Dining Out		
Water Bills			Papers/books		
Gas			Hobbies/sports		
Electricity			Entertainment		
Oil/Other fuel			Holidays		
Decoration/Repairs/ Maintenance			Clothing		
Telephone			Hairdressers		
Garden			**TOTAL**		
Renewal of house-hold equipment			**INSURANCE/ SAVINGS**		
Furniture, carpets etc			Motor		
TV &Video rental and licence			Household		
Food			Medical		
Drink			Life assurance		
Pets			Others		
TOTAL			**TOTAL**		
TRANSPORT			**MISC.**		
Car Tax			Presents		
Car maintenance			Dentists		
Car petrol/oil			Chemists		
AA/RAC			Day to day expenses		
Car replacement			Others		
TOTAL			**TOTAL**		
TOTAL COLUMN ONE			**TOTAL COLUMN TWO**		

MY TOTAL ANNUAL EXPENDITURE IS ESTIMATED AT £..................

This form is intended as a guide – be as accurate as possible and allow for inflation over the next 12 months. If anything be over-generous –you can always cut back

Risk Strategy

There are a number of considerations which must be borne in mind when devising an investment strategy, including personal investment preferences and existing investments; the purpose of the investment; the time frame; the tax position and degree of acceptable risk and the age of the client.

Investment type	Risk factor	
Technology and Telecoms European Smaller Companies North American Smaller Companies	10	Very Speculative
Japan Smaller Companies Global Emerging Markets Specialist Japan	9	Speculative
UK Smaller Companies Far East Excl Japan Europe Excl UK North America	8	Aggressive
Far East including Japan Europe Including UK Global Growth UK All Companies Active Managed	7	Realistic to Aggressive
UK Equity Income Balanced Managed	6	Realistic
UK Equity and Bond	5	Cautious to Realistic
Cautious Managed	4	Cautious
UK Other Bond Global Bond	3	Conservative
UK Index Linked Gilts UK Gilt Property/With Profits UK Corporate Bond	2	Very Conservative
Money Market	1	Ultra Conservative

8

Past Tense,
Future Perfect

The current retirement culture in the UK is complicated, and undergoing a process of dramatic change with increased longevity, changes in retirement age, and reductions in state pension provision.

But how did we get here?

In Europe, the whole issue of retirement is handled in a very relaxed manner. In Italy it seems to be quite normal for people working in the public sector to retire at 50 on a pension and promptly start another job. A similar situation can be found in France. In the USA, however, the situation is a lot different. In 1987, Congress passed an Act which, in general terms, allowed people to work beyond the age of 70. Of course, this exemplifies the American attitude to work, where people have less public holidays and less holiday times than in Europe. In this country we appear to fall between both these approaches.

It is not unusual to find people retiring before 60 and yet there is pressure for people to work beyond 65. On the other hand, age discrimination at work continues to be an issue.

For the future, the long-term diagnosis for retirees is not as good as it is for the current batch of retirees. Although people are living longer, the opportunities for a long retirement after work look set to become more remote, as the government seeks to push the retirement age further and further back. In addition, the reduction in state pension provision may make it difficult for some people to afford to stop working early. In the future this may result in future retirees having less chance to contemplate a long retirement. In this respect, the current generation of retirees need to make the most of this golden opportunity.

Traditionally after retiring from work people had a role awaiting them within the family, either as parents or grandparents (or both), but times have changed. This role for the older members in our society was fairly straightforward up to about 200 years ago. The family was the main basis of social existence, in which older members were seen as important members to be looked at for guidance and leadership.

Large families were the order of the day. But with the start of the Industrial Revolution, the relationships within the family changed quite dramatically. Large numbers of people moved off the land and into the towns and cities seeking work. Initially they brought their families with them into the urban environment. It was quite common to find parents and children living in the same street or nearby in the same area.

This situation lasted for some time but gradually started to break down as the family began to change with the different social pressures becoming evident within society. There was much more social mobility and children started to move away from their parents. Another feature of the breakdown of the family unit was the growth of divorce became common.

Inevitably, this caused a change of role for the older generation, and this has been particularly the case for the current generation of retirees. On the one hand, their help is still needed to look after grandchildren who seem to be arriving as they themselves are getting older, as siblings took on parenthood at later stages in life. On the other hand, the speed of technological changes in society has caused our knowledge and experience to become more redundant by the second according to our children.

These changes seem to have created a well of unhappiness for some members of the older generation. The traditional role seems to be disappearing without the replacement of a satisfactory alternative. Two possibilities seem to be available.

Perhaps the government of the day can be pressurised into providing a better environment – better concessionary services, in travel, healthcare or bigger pensions (some chance of that!).

Certainly the American experience with the more mature members of the population getting together to become a political force ('grey power') seems to offer a possible solution.

But up to now the British experience has not been very positive in terms of pensioner power. Perhaps the political will is not yet at a suitable temperature to produce such action, but we should caution the political parties not to continue to rely on our apathy, since it should not be taken for granted.

The other solution is for the mature generation to do their own thing. This, of course, has been one of the main themes of this book. We do not advocate a wholly selfish approach to life, but we do recommend that individuals take a conscious look and take control of their own destiny. So you have a choice, either to drift into the sunset, ignored and forgotten by the rest of society, or instead, take the opportunity to fully become yourselves. Doing what you want to do as valuable members of society. The choice is yours.

Keep life in perspective

At age 4	Success is	–	not wetting your pants
At age 12	Success is	–	having friends
At age 17	Success is	–	having a driving license.
At age 20	Success is	–	having sex
At age 35	Success is	–	having money
At age 50	Success is	–	having money
At age 60	Success is	–	having sex
At age 70	Success is	–	having a driving license
At age 75	Success is	–	having friends
At age 80	Success is	–	not wetting your pants.

'Now I must turn my questing violet eyes to 1969, my seventieth year. There really is no comment to make about that except perhaps 'Well, well.' 'Fancy' or 'Oh Fuck'

Noel Coward

There's a lot to be said for retirement
providing there's plenty to do
and assuming you're able to manage
on what you'll receive as your due.

It's when Friday's handshakes are over
and Monday arrives just the same that
you suddenly feel a back number
and this is the end of the game.

But it's only the end of a chapter
You've merely turned over a page
of a life story that you are unfolding
as you reach a particular stage.

Retirement is what you make it,
A time to relax and enjoy
opportunities no one has time for
while serving in someone's employ.

The secret's an inner contentment
That springs from a well ordered mind
Not sitting back in a corner
And leaving it all behind.

There are things to plan to live for;
ambitions still to fulfil.
Learning's an open door
for those with a positive will.

*(Extract from a poem by T.H.Offley
from Sutton Coldfeld)*

The Future

For people retiring now, the future has never looked brighter. 1984 has been and gone. Perhaps the next definitive novel about the future will have to be called '2084', although the notion of 'Big Brother' has been devalued somewhat.

To paraphrase an old Tory Prime Minister, people born after the war have always 'had it so good'. Because of the sheer numbers of the baby boomers, more hospitals had to be built to cater for their health. More schools had to be built to educate them. More houses had to be built to accommodate them and certainly more jobs had to be created to keep them employed.

Sarah Harper, Director of the Oxford Institute for Ageing maintains: 'By 2030 half the population of Europe will be over 50, with a predicted life expectancy at age 50 of another 40 years. Half of western Europe's population will be between 50 and 100 years old.' She also notes: 'The group aged 80 is the fastest growing age group in the world, with an annual growth rate of 3.9%.

In his book *The Age Wave,* Ken Dykwald puts an extremely convincing argument forward about the effect that this volume of human beings will have on the structure of society over the next few years. Because of the sheer numbers, this tsunami of energy, wisdom and experience, will demand a voice in how society operates and who calls the shots.

He poses the focal question: 'While the strength of the senses may be lessening, what if the powers of the mind, the heart and the spirit are rising? Becoming more than we have ever been before is the point of extended life.'

The 'grey pound' will have an enormous impact on business and in the way consumers behave. The whole focus of advertising and marketing will have to shift from its current obsession with youth, superficial beauty, and the immediate satisfaction of immature needs.

In those classifications so beloved of market research agencies, there is a new category of 'WOOFs' – well off older people. These people, over fifty, own 80% of the nation's wealth and are set to spend £46 billion per year by the year 2008 on consumer goods.

Mature consumers will be more discerning and sceptical of advertising claims.

They will demand more detailed information and will be more discerning with their substantial spending power. They will no longer be considered to be suitable targets, only for stair-lifts and walk-in baths. But they will demand more significant messages in travel, fashion, technology and leisure products. They will be dismissive of the claims of the snake-oil salesmen in the health and beauty business with their flimsy claims to everlasting beauty and health. They will have the enormous financial clout to develop a new marketplace where they are no longer on the periphery but are at the centre of any advertising and business initiative that has a chance of any kind of commercial success.

Organisations as we know them in their current form are in their death throes.

Although many have made drastic efforts to keep pace with the changing environment, one of the main areas that they have failed to adapt to is the needs of their own employees. In the future, organisations will have to adopt a more segmented approach to their employers. They will need to cater for their younger members. They will still need avenues for promotion and advancement, but they will also have to take into account the younger workers' approach to the work/life balance. By the same rule they will need to provide for the more mature worker, who may not be too interested in advancement and promotion, but will generally be more interested in the quality of life. For these people, sabbaticals, secondments and the phasing of retirement will be more important than climbing the greasy pole. In the current organisations, it seems that one size fits all and no matter how they re-structure or re-engineer they will be doomed to failure because of this basic flaw.

Similarly, the full impact of these demographic changes has not yet been seen in the political arena. Some commentators maintain that there is already an Age War in existence as well-heeled seniors compete for resources and services with a cash strapped younger generation. They are calling it the 'Battle of the Birthdays' or the 'Clash of the Generations'. A battle between a generation who have had the advantages of the property boom, a stable economy and almost full employment on the one hand, and a future generation impoverished by debt incurred in gaining an education, afflicted by house price inflation, and unable to get on the property ladder. The irony is that this younger generation will be funding the pensions of the older generation while their own pension hopes remain a dream.

With this substantial increase in the numbers of people over 50, this will tear asunder the traditional political arena. It will shatter the cosy political liaisons between the three main parties. It will traverse traditional party loyalties and once harnessed could restructure the whole political landscape as we know it.

Based in Washington, The 'Grey Panthers' or to give them their real name, the 'Consultation of Older and Younger Adults for Social Change', are a group who are having an increasingly profound effect on American political life. They are an energetic lobbying group and have already had a significant impact on political decisions.

They have had significant achievements in healthcare, taxation and social security as well as wider global issues. Any legislation that may effect the older generation is closely scrutinised and if necessary criticized and alternative viewpoints raised.

The new activists will have one main asset over all their rivals. In addition to experience, wisdom and, dare one say it, common sense, they will have an abundance of time to devote to harnessing this new-found power.

They will have time to harass their local MPs. They will have time to write letters and e-mails. They will have time to organise pressure groups. They might even have time to read the European Constitution, which would be a great advantage over many professional politicians. They will have time to devote to public relations and all the other activities that are needed for any successful political initiative.

Over the years there have been many successful initiatives that have overcome sexism and racism. There is absolutely no reason why this movement cannot overcome ageism in all its insidious forms.

The building of a society that celebrates age is not an act of charity. Fighting ageism and all that it stands for is not about 'them and us' – it is 'us and us'.

Every single one of us will be old too, even politicians. Now is the time to act. Bend the ears of these politicians and we will all share the benefits. We owe it to the generations before us, who fought to overcome the scourge of early death so that we can now enjoy the right to become old.

Over the years there have been scores of mature protestors, mainly women, who have elected to serve a prison sentence, rather than pay what they consider to be an iniquitous Council Tax. They demonstrate the courage and conviction of the early Suffragettes and are an example to all mature revolutionaries.

The nation's hearts were warmed and hackles rose when that gentleman Walter Wolfgang was physically ejected from the Labour Party conference for heckling in 2005. He shouted 'Nonsense' when Jack Straw was making excuses for the Iraq War, when he was set upon by two thugs double his size and half his age and removed from the auditorium.

Veteran peace campaigner, eighty-two-year-old Walter, who escaped Nazi Germany in 1937, is a hero and is a shining example of mature militancy.

So that is it…. Go to it…. Raise your banners, slowly. You have nothing to lose but your zimmer frames.

'When people ask me what I would like for my eighty-fifth birthday
– I tell them – a paternity suite.'

George Burns

There must be something extremely satisfying for the couple of fit, active octogenarians, who have just driven a camper van through Nepal. We have all read about the seventy-seven-year-old lady getting a degree in Mathematics or the sixty-eight-year-old gentleman running the London Marathon for the first time. As we have mentioned earlier in this book, these people have more energy and drive in their little finger than many teenagers have in their whole body.

The world is full of mature people who are pushing the boundaries of their experiences, be it in travel, education, sport, technology or other areas of achievement.

Growing old is mandatory; growing up is optional. Fundamentally it seems to be a question of relinquishing old, debilitating habits and developing new, positive ones.

'The unfortunate thing about this world is that the good habits are far easier to give up than the bad ones.'

Somerset Maughan

When you talk to these people there are various themes that keep re-occurring in their testimonies.

Shining through all these remarkable people is their attitude towards the process of ageing. They will say that age is in the mind. They have a very positive, yet realistic attitude to ageing. OK, they are never going to break any athletic records, but they say many of the factors that limit activity in ageing are merely imagined. They point to a difference between biological age and functional age. They actively challenge the stereotypes associated with the ageing process.

Aristotle maintained that there are two trends of thinking that older people adopt. Firstly they become more self-centred. Every event is judged as to what direct effect it will have on the individual.

Secondly they become more rigid in their thinking patterns. They rely on tried and tested patterns of thought that have seen them through many, many years.

Once we are aware of this, we can take steps to annul or at least diminish these effects.

We can become less self-centred, being genuinely interested in other people's lives, interests and opinions. We can also resist any tendency to rigidity in thought processes, being more flexible and adaptable, more receptive and creative and willing to embrace new ideas and points of view.

Successful retirees are inspired by the achievements of many statesmen and thinkers who produced their most effective work in their mature years. People like Churchill, of course, Einstein, George Washington, George Bernard Shaw, Gandhi and Picasso

– and remember the enormous impact Nelson Mandela has had on the world scene since his release from prison. Ronald Reagan was still ruling the world from the White House in his 70's – or at least he thought he was.

The current incumbent, the equally hallucinatory George W. Bush, who added to the English lexicon when he insisted he had been 'misunderestimated', is 60. Some people may not consider him to be the ideal role model for the mature person. Most of the world's leading statesmen, religious leaders and Nobel prize-winners are eligible for a British bus pass and even our own dear Queen is still cutting the mustard in her 80s.

It beggars the imagination to think that the next Pope could be a Justin Timberlake look alike, with snake hips, a penchant for skateboarding and a tendency to wear his biretta back to front.

In 2003, at 60 years of age, Sir Ranulph Fiennes ran 7 marathons in 7 days on 7 continents – this, despite having suffered a major heart attack and a double bypass operation earlier in the same year.

A glance at *The Guinness Book of Records* shows a few choice entries:

Senator John Glenn. Oldest male astronaut at age 77 and 103 days when he went up in the U.S Space shuttle Discovery October 29 1998.

George Blair, Winter Gardens Florida oldest water skier at age 87 and 18 days in Winter Gardens, Florida February 10 2002.

Otto Comanus. Australia. Oldest windsurfer when he retired at age 89 in 1986.

Flossie Bennett 97, United Kingdom, oldest bridesmaid since 1999.

Now there's an idea for you, why not get into *The Guinness Book of Records*?

In the world of arts and entertainment people like the Three Tenors, the Buena Vista Social Club, Kiri Te Kanawa and Tony Bennett continue to captivate audiences world wide.

Performers like, Cliff Richard (Zimmer Holiday?), Tom Jones, Paul McCartney (Now I'm sixty-four?), Bob Dillon, Joan Baez, Cher, Dolly Parton, and the Rolling Stones still strut their stuff on the world stage.

Robert Redford, Jack Nicholson, Michael and his father Kirk Douglas, Rolf Harris, Goldie Hawn, Diane Keaton, Susan Sarandon, Jane Fonda, Helen Mirren Judie Dench, Maggie Smith and Joanna Lumley are still extending the boundaries of their art and talent.

Even as we are writing this, Clint Eastwood has just won not one but two Oscars. He is seventy-six and in his acceptance speech, he gifts credit to his mother, who is ninety-six and in the audience.

The popularity of the 'Women's Institute' calendar and the acclaim given to the subsequent film 'Calendar Girls' is ample testimony to the beauty of women of a certain age. It is difficult imagining a 'Men's Institute' calendar having even a quarter of this appeal. Speaking of calendars, Sophia Loren is currently set to appear on a Pirelli calendar.

> 'I do not believe we grow older, I think what happens early in life is that at a certain age one stands still and stagnates.'
>
> *T. S. Eliot*

Another recurring theme from happy retirees is that they never stop learning. Some report that the older they get, the more they realise how little they know.

They have enquiring minds, always interested in broadening their horizons. They are not imprisoned by their experience and previous knowledge. They are receptive to new ideas and points of view. Above all they have maintained their sense of curiosity.

Medical evidence indicates that the brain is receptive to new ideas and experiences. It is curious and there is evidence that stimulated brain neurones will actually re-grow.

If we actively use our minds, especially with new topics and interests, we can enhance our mental abilities well into the future. The brain does not deteriorate as a result of growing older, but through not being properly nourished and used.

'The art of being wise is the art of knowing what to overlook.'

William James

Another secret of success in the transition seems to be to surround yourself with like-minded people. Successful retirees limit and even avoid too much contact with people who want to dwell in the past – people who hanker after 'the good old days' and lament 'the current state of the nation', who hate current music and fashion, values and mores and think the younger generation are out of control. Our successful people seek out the younger people and value their opinions. Most of all, they *become good listeners and they are prepared to listen to the younger generation and people from different backgrounds and cultures. They realise that younger people do not relish any unsolicited advice and are frugal with their counsel.*

They either accept or reject things modern on their own merit.

They keep abreast of current trends and cultural activities. They are alive to new experiences and perspectives. In fact they actually seek them out.

Also, they retain a great sense of humour. They have a great capacity for laughter, and a propensity for having fun. They are attractive people and nice to be around. Much of this laughter is at their own expense, always an ability that gives everything an appropriate sense of proportion.

Most of all, however, the single most important feature of the successful retiree is that they do live in the present moment. They have enjoyed the past, and they have some really pleasant memories but do not wish to dwell there. They have some plans for the future, but they do not plan their lives away, waiting for some future enjoyment. They enjoy every second of the here and now.

The Eskimos have a saying:

> 'Yesterday is ashes, tomorrow is wood. It is only today when the fire burns brightly.'

They are action people. They do not spend their lives on holiday on the 'Someday Isle' or wait around until they get 'a round tuit'. They are 'doers' who 'seize the day'.

> 'Action may not always bring happiness, but there is no happiness without action.'

> *Benjamin Disraeli*

To live a full life in retirement is one thing, to live a rich and happy one is an entirely different matter. The key seems to be not to confuse 'Activity' or 'Standard of Living' with the 'Quality of Life'.

They do not want to leave this world with any nagging feeling about what would have happened if only…. They want to slip off this mortal coil with a bang, with a song and a bottle of champagne in the sure knowledge that they have at least given life a full go. This is not a rehearsal and life is not a spectator sport.

Some people die at 50 but are not buried until they are 75.

Anon

As they say, the best way to go is just after your 98th birthday, from a swift heart attack, being chased by an irate husband and a worried bank manager.

Further Reading

The Age of Unreason by Charles Handy, published in 1995 by Random House Business Books

Age Wave, by Ken Dychtwald, published in 1990 by Bantam Doubleday Dell Publishing Group

The Chance to Live More Than Once – Developing Future Lives and Careers, by Barry Curnow and John McLean Fox, published in 1997 by Management Books 2000

Inheritance Tax Simplified, by Tony Granger, published in 2007 by Management Books 2000

The Joy of Laziness, by Michaela Axt-Gaderman and Peter Axt, published in 2005 by Bloomsbury Publilshing

Pensions Simplified, by Tony Granger, published in 2007 by Management Books 2000

You… Unlimited, by Colin McCrudden, Adrian Bourne and Christopher Lyons, published in 2005 by Management Books 2000